For Evy
With much love
and admiration —

Peggy and Ralph

June 12, 2022

St Cuthbert

His Life and Cult in Medieval Durham

ST CUTHBERT

HIS LIFE AND CULT IN
MEDIEVAL DURHAM

Dominic Marner

THE BRITISH LIBRARY

For my children
Pascale and Sudesh

First published in 2000 by
The British Library
96 Euston Road
London NW1 2DB

© 2000 in text Dominic Marner
© 2000 in illustrations, The British Library and other named copyright owners

British Library Cataloguing in Publication Data
A catalogue record for this book is available from The British Library

ISBN 0 7123 4686 4

Designed and typeset by Andrew Shoolbred
Colour origination by South Sea International Press
Printed in Hong Kong by South Sea International Press

Contents

Note   6

Acknowledgements   6

List of Plates   7

Introduction   9

Chapter 1: Cuthbert and Lindisfarne   11

Chapter 2: Cuthbert and Durham   20

Chapter 3: The *Life* of St Cuthbert   37

Conclusion   54

THE PLATES   57-103

Abbreviations   104

Appendix   105

Notes   106

Select Bibliography   110

Index   111

Note

Translations are taken from Bertram Colgrave's translation of Bede's *Life* of Saint Cuthbert published in: *Two Lives of Saint Cuthbert*, Cambridge, 1940 and *Bede's Ecclesiastical History of the English People*, Bertram Colgrave and R.A.B. Mynors eds, Oxford, 1969, reprinted with corrections 1991.

Acknowledgments

I would like to thank the following individuals for their encouragement, comments and criticisms: Michelle Brown, William Noel, T.A. Heslop, C.M. Kauffmann, Malcolm Baker, Alan Piper, Roger Norris, John Mitchell, John Osborne, Alan Thacker, Carol Davidson, Kathleen Lane, Matthew Moran, Cesare Poppi, Christopher Norton, William Aird, Bernard Meehan, Roger Stalley, Malcolm Thurlby, Eric Fernie, Simon Pennington, David Way and Elaine Wright. Lara Speicher of British Library Publishing, and the anonymous readers of the book, enhanced the text greatly.

For their co-operation in this project I would like to express my gratitude to the following libraries and their staff: The British Library (London); Dean and Chapter Library (Durham); the Biblioteca Apostolica Vaticana (Vatican City); the Bodleian Library (Oxford); Cambridge University Library (Cambridge); Trinity College Library (Cambridge); and the Bibliothèque Nationale (Paris). Trinity College, Dublin, and the University of East Anglia, Norwich, provided the necessary institutional support for the successful completion of the book while research grants from the Institute of Historical Research (London) and the Social Science and Humanities Research Council of Canada enabled the work to be finished.

Finally, for their unfailing support, I would like to thank Nalini Persram, Terence Marner and Veronica Marner.

List of Plates

BL Yates Thompson Ms 26:

1.   [Preface]   Monk kissing the feet of Cuthbert, 1v
2.   [Preface]   A tonsured, seated scribe, thought to be Bede, 2
3.   [Chp. 2]   Initial 'P', 7v
4.   [Chp. 3]   Cuthbert praying besides the river Tyne, 10v
5.   [Chp. 3]   Two monks praying at the monastery of Tynemouth, 11
6.   [Chp. 5]   A horse discovers food for the saint, 14
7.   [Chp. 6]   Cuthbert embraced by Boisil at Melrose Abbey, 16
8.   [Chp. 7]   Cuthbert washes an angel's feet, 17v
9.   [Chp. 7]   The miraculous loaves from paradise, 18
10. [Chp. 8]   Cuthbert talking to Boisil, 21
11. [Chp. 9]   Cuthbert preaching, 22v
12. [Chp. 10]   Cuthbert praying in the sea and his feet wiped by otters, 24
13. [Chp. 11]   Cuthbert in a boat, 26
14. [Chp. 11]   Cuthbert with a dolphin, 26v
15. [Chp. 12]   A fish is shared out, 28v
16. [Chp. 13]   Cuthbert driving away a demon, 30
17. [Chp. 14]   Cuthbert praying at the fire, 31v
18. [Chp. 15]   Cuthbert heals the wife of Hildmaer, 33v
19. [Chp. 16]   Cuthbert teaching the monks at Lindisfarne, 35v
20. [Chp. 17]   Cuthbert making his hermitage with the help of an angel, 39
21. [Chp. 18]   Cuthbert digging with a monk, 41
22. [Chp. 19]   Cuthbert expelling birds, 42v
23. [Chp. 20]   Crows pick thatch and bring lard to Cuthbert, 44
24. [Chp. 21]   Cuthbert discovers the roof beam, 45v
25. [Chp. 22]   Cuthbert with a crowd, 47
26. [Chp. 23]   Aelfflaed cured by Cuthbert's girdle, 48v
27. [Chp. 24]   Aelfflaed meets Cuthbert, 50v
28. [Chp. 24]   Ecgfrith visits Cuthbert, 51
29. [Chp. 24]   Cuthbert at synod, 53v
30. [Chp. 25]   Cuthbert blessing water and a cure, 54
31. [Chp. 27]   Cuthbert and Ecgfrith's widow, 55v
32. [Chp. 29]   Healing a gesith's wife, 58v
33. [Chp. 30]   Healing a girl, 60
34. [Chp. 31]   Healing a man, 61
35. [Chp. 33]   Healing a child, 62v

8

36.   [Chp. 34]   Fall from a tree, 63v

37.   [Chp. 34]   Cuthbert's vision, 64

38.   [Chp. 35]   Cuthbert passing wine, 66

39.   [Chp. 38]   Cuthbert takes a monk on to his boat, 71v

40.   [Chp. 39]   The death of Cuthbert, 73

41.   [Chp. 40]   Signaling the death by torches, 74v

42.   [Chp. 42]   Discovery of the incorrupt body, 77

43.   [Chp. 44]   Sick man healed at the tomb, 79

44.   [Chp. 45]   Man healed by shoes, 80

45.   Historia ecclesiastica, bk. iv, 31–32

Cuthbert's arm emerges from the tomb to cure paralytic, 83

46.   Historia ecclesiastica, bk. iv, 32

Youth's eye healed, 84v

Introduction

A hermit, prior and then bishop to the monastic community at Lindisfarne, Cuthbert became, upon his death in 687, one of the most important medieval saints in Europe and one of the foremost saints of medieval England. His importance is demonstrated by the large number of pilgrims attracted to his shrine and by the number of gifts bestowed upon him by pilgrims and Kings alike. During his lifetime he was visited by Ecgfrith, King of Northumbria (670–85) at his hermitage on Farne Island and, furthermore, his popularity with the nobility even extended beyond his death when, during the ninth century, Cuthbert miraculously 'appeared' to King Alfred at Glastonbury. His shrine was later visited by subsequent kings of England, Aethelstan in 934, Edmund in 945 and Cnut in 1027. Lands and other treasures were bestowed upon Cuthbert by Aethelstan and others inevitably making Cuthbert's monastic community one of the most powerful and wealthy in England.

Indeed, Cuthbert was considered perhaps the most popular saint in England prior to the death of Thomas Becket in 1170. By the late eleventh century his feast days were celebrated in many monasteries throughout England and Europe. His popularity in Europe is apparent by the number of his *Lives* (or *Vitae*) which were carefully penned by continental scribes in order that their monastic communities should have a copy. In addition, his name appears in many European Martyrologies, liturgical books containing readings on the lives of the saints, and in all parts of England many churches were dedicated to him. To this day his shrine in Durham Cathedral and his home in Lindisfarne receive many pilgrims and visitors.

The cult of the saints in the Middle Ages encompassed the practice of certain rituals associated with the saint's physical remains and the establishment of important feast days. In addition, biographies of the holy person were written (*Lives*) and shrines and buildings were constructed in order that the saint should be properly housed and a focal point be provided for pilgrims to visit and venerate the saint. Also, objects, such as the remains of the saint, beautiful books, vestments and metalwork were displayed in order to embellish the shrine and further testify to the saint's special character. Cuthbert was the particular focus of a great deal of artistic and architectural production. The Lindisfarne Gospels in The British Library, the Cuthbert Gospel of St John, the seventh-century gold and garnet pendant cross, King Aethelstan's gift of vestments and the coffin itself, all housed in Durham Cathedral Treasury, and the London *Life* of Saint Cuthbert (British Library, Yates Thompson MS 26) (PLATES 1–46) are just some of the beautiful and historically significant objects inspired by Cuthbert and associated with his following.

Cuthbert teaching the monks at Lindisfarne. Detail from Plate 19. BL Yates Thompson MS26, f.35v.

Saints were important figures in the Middle Ages, not simply because they acted as spiritual role models for the people and performed curative and other miracles, but also because they helped in forming a sense of unity and cohesion to regional and even national communities and provided these groups of people with a sense of purpose and strength. In this respect, Cuthbert is a poignant example. His *Life*, or more accurately his *Lives*, were changed subtly over time to reflect the concerns of those interested in fostering his cult at critical moments.

The purpose of this book is to examine the cult of Cuthbert, in particular in the late twelfth century – a time of great importance in the history of the cult and Durham – and to assess the material culture produced at this time as a result of the efforts by the monastic community and the Bishop to revitalize the cult. The idea that Cuthbert could be instrumentally manipulated and transformed in the interests of promoting Durham, the North and his cult is the central theme of this book. Moreover, it is one that is crucial for understanding the relationship between Cuthbert and Durham during the twelfth century.

Chapter 1

Cuthbert and Lindisfarne

Cuthbert and the early cult

St Cuthbert has been the focus of much scholarly attention and the object of popular affection ever since his death. His life was one of cloistered monastic observance and isolated prayer combined with pastoral responsibilities, and the community at Lindisfarne recognized his saintly character and helped nurture his reputation as a miracle worker and holy person even during his lifetime. As a result, Cuthbert became the focus of one of the most famous and enduring cults of the Middle Ages.

Eleven years after his death in 687 his body was found incorrupt in his coffin. Almost immediately three *Lives* were written. The first *Life* was written by an anonymous author[1] and was soon supplemented by two other versions of his life written by Bede (673–735), the great Northumbrian historian (PLATE 2).[2] The *Lives* were very firmly rooted in the geography of Northumbria and more specifically the island community of monks.

The first, anonymous *Life* was probably written about 700 and was most likely a first-hand account of many of the events of Cuthbert's life.[3] However, like many hagiographical works, the author chose to incorporate sections of other saints' *Lives* into the account, an act of plagiarism not out of step with contemporary practice. All saints' *Lives* have a certain similarity to them, simply because they all, to some degree, reflect the notion that a saint should imitate Christ, a point made by the sixth-century Pope, Gregory of Tours.[4] However, this anonymous author was not concerned with the saintly aspects of Cuthbert's life and character; his intention was not to depict Cuthbert preaching moral codes of conduct, but rather he wished to portray him as a miracle-worker.[5] In other words, in this first *Life* of Cuthbert the promotion and establishment of Cuthbert as an intercessor between Man and God, as manifested in the miraculous, was the primary focus of the author.

Bede wrote both a metrical and a prose *Life*. His approach to the prose *Life*, which was written by 721, was somewhat different from his earlier metrical version.[6] He included additional passages in the prose *Life* which served to portray Cuthbert's personality in more detail than he had done in the Metrical *Life* and to define his roles as prior, hermit and bishop, aspects of his life which previously had been glossed over in favour of the stories of him as a miracle worker.[7] Bede presented the saint as conscientiously performing all the duties of bishop, such as ordaining priests, conferring the veil on royal postulants, visiting the many villages of the diocese, and ministering to those people afflicted with the plague (PLATE 34).[8]

The implication of the three-dimensional portrayal of Cuthbert as prior, hermit and bishop was that potentially any one of these roles could be appropriated by particular persons or groups in later times in order to support their specific ideological requirements, although this was not Bede's original intention. For instance, it was more potent at certain times to remind a monastic audience of Cuthbert as hermit or Cuthbert as prior, rather than Cuthbert as bishop. Likewise, the way in which Cuthbert was portrayed, as monk, prior or bishop, might say something about the person or persons who wished to portray him in such a guise.

Bede also changed the structure of Cuthbert's *Life*. The anonymous author had structured his *Life* into four books each concerned with a period of the saint's life. This four-part arrangement mirrored that of the much-admired *Life* of St Martin (316/35–397) and of St Benedict (*c*.480–550) and indicates a desire on the part of the author to create a similar monumental and important *Life* for St Cuthbert. Bede changed this arrangement and instead adopted a forty-six chapter structure for both his metrical and prose *Lives*.

Walter Berschin, an eminent literary historian, has proposed that Bede must have been aware of St Augustine's commentary on the name 'Adam' and his related homily on the subject of the forty-six years needed to build the temple in Jerusalem.[9] St Augustine noticed that the Greek names for the four quarters of the world, Anatole, Dysis, Arctos and Mesembria, produced the acronym for the word ADAM. And, furthermore, the numerical equivalent for the word ADAM in Greek is forty-six. Bede expanded upon Augustine's number symbolism to elaborate and comment upon St John's remark that the forty-six years needed to rebuild the temple was actually a reference to the 'temple of his body'. Bede concluded that it took forty-six days from conception for a body and soul to be formed.[10] He therefore felt that the number forty-six and the notion of a perfect man were somehow connected and Berschin suggests that it was this association that led Bede consciously to adopt forty-six chapters in his metrical *Life* of Cuthbert and to maintain that number of chapters in the prose *Life*.

According to Bede's *Life*, Cuthbert entered the priory at Melrose Abbey, on the Scottish borders, as a boy in 651. He studied under the tutelage of the abbot Boisil, himself a revered holy man (PLATES 7 and 10), and was soon ordained a priest, after which he travelled extensively throughout Northumbria preaching the Word, meeting his fellow countrymen and administering the sacraments.

Cuthbert soon gained a certain reputation for holiness, and his travels took him to Ripon, near York, where he helped to found a new monastery, but soon after he returned to Melrose where he became Prior. Then, in 664, he was made

Prior of Lindisfarne. The island of Lindisfarne is cut off from the world at high tide, so the location alone would naturally have given him a more contemplative existence. Nevertheless, Cuthbert wanted even further isolation. In 676 he moved to Farne Island, totally cut off from both the mainland and Lindisfarne, and built a small hermitage where he lived in quiet prayer (PLATES 20–24). The importance of the physical environment of Farne is reflected in the great number of stories in Bede's *Life* related to the geography and wildlife of this place as well as the unpredictable nature of the weather.

His reputation, even in this remote place, grew greater and many made what must have been a perilous journey to see him. Because of his reputation as a holy man the community of monks at Lindisfarne naturally wanted him as their bishop. They therefore elected him unanimously as bishop at a 'synod' at which Ecgfrith, King of the Northumbrians from 672 to 685, and Archbishop Theodore of Canterbury (*c.*612–90) presided. Cuthbert had become accustomed to the secluded life on Farne Island and was reluctant to become bishop. It took a considerable entourage, which included Ecgfrith himself, to go to the island in 684 in order to try to persuade him to accept the election (PLATE 28). Only when Cuthbert was taken, 'shedding many tears, from his sweet retirement', to the synod was he overcome by the unanimous will of his brethren and decided to submit to the 'yoke of the bishopric' (PLATE 29). He was accordingly consecrated in 685. After

FIG. I. A view of St Cuthbert's Island from Lindisfarne.

two years, however, he gave up his pastoral duties as bishop because of ill health, and returned to Farne where he continued his preferred solitude. He died on 20 March 687, probably in his mid-fifties (PLATES 40 and 41; FIG. 2).

Although Cuthbert had throughout his life chosen a path of simplicity and retirement from the world, his cult, from the beginning, was marked by extravagant splendour. Despite his desire for a simple internment on Farne Island, his body was taken to Lindisfarne for burial. As historian Alan Thacker has pointed out, his enshrinement was very opulent. 'In death', he says, 'he was honoured like an Emperor.' Cuthbert was wrapped in a beautiful and precious cloth given to him by Abbess Verca; his body was clothed in fine garments including a white dalmatic apparently similar to those in which contemporary archbishops of Ravenna were buried.[11] A silk chasuble and a gold embroidered alb were included as was the gold and garnet pectoral cross possibly worn by Cuthbert in his lifetime and now housed in Durham Cathedral Treasury (FIG. 3).[12] Finally, his body and the precious textiles and metalwork were placed in an elaborate wooden sarcophagus upon which were carved images of Christ and the four evangelists' symbols, the archangels Michael and Gabriel, the Virgin and child, the twelve apostles and a further five more archangels. Eleven years later his sarcophagus was opened, as was the custom, in order to gather the bones and place them above ground in a shrine, a process then equivalent to canonization. His body was found to be miraculously incorrupt, which provided confirmation of his saintly status (PLATE 42).

FIG. 2. Signaling the death of Cuthbert. *Life* of St Cuthbert, Oxford, University College MS 165, p.113.

FIG. 3. Cuthbert's Pectoral Cross

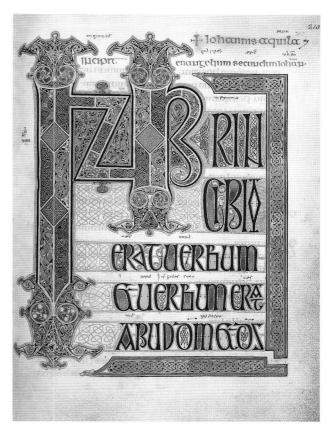

15

FIG. 4. Evangelist St John. Lindisfarne Gospels, BL Cotton MS Nero D.iv, 209v.

FIG. 5. Decorated initial page beginning the Gospel of St John. Lindisfarne Gospels, BL Cotton MS Nero D.iv, 211.

It was during the eleven-year interval between his death and first exhumation that the Lindisfarne Gospels (British Library, Cotton MS Nero D.iv) were probably written and illuminated (FIGS 4 and 5).[13] This volume is now on display at The British Library and is considered one of the great masterpieces of manuscript painting. A colophon in the manuscript reads: 'Eadfrith, Bishop of the Lindisfarne church, originally wrote this book, for God and for Saint Cuthbert.' This book, with its beautiful script, its marvelously intricate decoration and stunning full-page illuminations was made (according to Aldred who wrote the colophon sometime after 970) in Cuthbert's honour.

In 793 the monastic community at Lindisfarne was raided by Vikings and the monks had to flee temporarily. They returned to Lindisfarne where they remained relatively peacefully until 875 when Bishop Eardwulf (d.899) decided that it was too hostile an environment given the continuing, vigorous attacks by the Vikings on other nearby monasteries in Northumbria. He took the relics of Cuthbert and other treasures, including the Lindisfarne Gospels, and the

FIG. 6. King Aethelstan presenting a manuscript to Cuthbert.
Cambridge Corpus Christi College MS 183, 1.

Lindisfarne community then travelled around Northumbria for seven years seeking an appropriate home for their patron saint. The very physical presence of
Cuthbert, in all areas of the kingdom of Northumbria, both while alive and after
his death, is a fascinating example of the way in which the corporeal presence of
a saint somehow helps sanctify a geographical region and affirms and strengthens

its boundaries.[14] This seven years of wandering was chronicled by the twelfth-century historian Symeon of Durham who recounts that after an aborted attempt to travel to Ireland the monks decided to settle at Chester-le-Street, near Durham. The community remained there between 883 and 995 during which time King Aethelstan (924–39) visited the shrine made to house Cuthbert's relics and bestowed on the community the marvelous vestments which were discovered in 1827 when the tomb was opened for inspection. He also gave a book containing the *Life of Cuthbert* to the community, which is thought to be the manuscript preserved in Cambridge Corpus Christi College depicting on its frontispiece Aethelstan presenting the book to Cuthbert (FIG. 6).

In 995, the community of monks moved to their present home on the site of Durham Cathedral, thereby initiating Durham's long-lived and important connection with Cuthbert. In 1083 Durham's monastic community was established by William of St Calais (Bishop between 1080–96) and he began the process of creating the magnificent cathedral.

Cuthbert and the North

Cuthbert and his cult were extremely important not only for Durham and the monastic community, but for the region as a whole and for the kingdom of Northumbria. His cult generated a great deal of material culture such as books, metalwork, architecture, and sculpture, it transformed the liturgical calendar of the religious and it provided the population of Northumbria with a saintly individual to help, protect and comfort them.

The practice of using patron saints as a means to cement a region or people together was not uncommon in the Middle Ages, and St Cuthbert provides an excellent example of just such a practice. The initial desire to elevate Cuthbert to saintly status was directly linked with the struggle for independence and hegemony of the Bernician kings in the late seventh century over their rival neighbours, the Deirians.[15] By the mid-sixth century these two dynasties dominated the geographical boundaries of Northumbria. The dividing line between the two dynasties was the River Tees; the Bernicians controlled land north of the Tees, while the Deirians had charge of land south of the river. The two dynasties were in constant conflict as control of Northumbria fluctuated from Deirian to Bernician between the mid-sixth and mid-seventh centuries. One of the most important Bernician Kings, Oswald (605–642), not only unified Northumbria under his rule, but also helped to establish Christianity in the North, becoming one of the first royal saints of Anglo-Saxon England. His head, arms and hands were severed from his body upon his death and were later taken as relics to the churches at Lindisfarne and Bamburgh, and by the twelfth century his head rested next to Cuthbert's body in the sarcophagus at the eastern end of Durham Cathedral.

As Alan Thacker has suggested, Cuthbert was promoted as the national saint of the Northumbrian kingdom in the same way as St Martin had been in Gaul.[16] Cuthbert's worldly connections with the Bernician kings made him a prime candidate for such an honour, and the rapid mythologizing of Cuthbert and the popularity of his cult were clear signs of the support he received from the Northumbrian kings.

Northumbrian identity played an important part in the way in which the North perceived itself throughout the Middle Ages, and still does even to this day. According to Helen Jewell, an historian of English identity, the division between the North and the South is not an invention of recent times but is literally 'as old as the hills'.[17] The geographical dividing line was, and still is, the Humber; those to the North were considered Northumbrians and those to the South, Southumbrians.

Eddius Stephanus, the biographer of St Wilfrid (634–709) and contemporary of Bede, also knew of the division imposed by the Humber. In his *Life of Wilfrid* he compared affairs in the North and South of England and alluded to the division in remarks such as 'in all kingdoms both sides of the Humber'.[18] On occasion he even identified himself as a Northumbrian (which he was not), as when he referred to Wulfhere of Mercia stirring up 'all the southern nations against our own'.[19]

Alfred the Great also noted the differences on either side of the Humber. In his preface to the *Pastoral Care* he lamented the fact that very few men 'this side of the Humber' could understand the divine services in English, or translate a single letter from Latin into English, and then went on to say that neither could many 'beyond' (the Humber).[20] However, it is not clear if he was referring to those who lived north of the Tyne beyond the Danelaw.

Until the end of the ninth century the kinds of comments made about the North-South divide were centred upon the political realities of the day and reflected the geographic composition of early Britain. However, with Asser, the biographer of King Alfred (871–99), the Northumbrians began to be ascribed with a distinctive set of inherent characteristics, in the same way that chroniclers attributed to the Normans their natural predilection towards cunning and deceit. Asser relates how 'a great dispute, fomented by the devil, had arisen among the Northumbrians, as always happens to a people which has incurred the wrath of God.'[21] This remark removed the Northumbrians from the abstract geo-political realm to that of the perceived natural habits of mind and thought of a 'people' (*gens*).

Writing in the twelfth century, Henry of Huntingdon remarked upon the Northumbrians' 'usual fickleness' with respect to their rulers,[22] and then went on to add that 'the Northumbrians are never long submissive to the same master'.[23]

William of Malmesbury, another twelfth-century chronicler, described the Northumbrian people as 'ripe for rebellion' and 'a ferocious race'.[24] He also described differences in their dialect.[25] The modern historian Marjorie Chibnall has described Northumbria as historically 'resolutely separatist' and as a 'sturdily independent region'.[26] Perhaps this 'separatism', if it can be described as such, was partly the result of the intermediary geographic position Northumbria occupied between England and Scotland and the resulting devastation the Northumbrians had encountered by both English and Scottish invasions.

The attention to the geography and environment of Farne, Lindisfarne and the whole of Northumbria that one finds in the *Lives* of Cuthbert placed him firmly in a northern landscape and provided geographical and topographical connections between the people of the region and their saint, thereby strengthing his power as a unifying symbol of the region.

Cuthbert was, however, more than just a symbol. A great deal of land and territory was given to the community of monks who had Cuthbert as their patron saint by King Aethelstan and others, and these land holdings came to be known as the Patrimony of St Cuthbert.[27] By the early twelfth century, those who lived on 'St Cuthbert's land' were identified as *Haliwerfolc*, or 'people of the saint' as it has recently been translated.[28] As William Aird, a historian of Durham, has recently argued, 'by extension, the land that they occupied became recognized as a geographical entity'. The *Haliwerfolc* were rather disparate peoples, not necessarily bonded by ethnicity or politics, but the unifying factor of their lives was the shrine and land of St Cuthbert. This provided them with a tremendous sense of cohesion and identity. In the imagination and daily life of 'the people of the saint', the land of Northumbria became integrated into the very idea of Cuthbert.

Chapter 2

Cuthbert and Durham

The twelfth-century cult at Durham

If the Lindisfarne Gospels can be considered one of the finest examples of medieval book-making, the Cathedral at Durham must be considered one of the most impressive medieval buildings (FIG. 7). Just as the Lindisfarne Gospels were made for Cuthbert, so the Cathedral was built to honour him and to house his body and associated relics.

By the late eleventh century Cuthbert's relics were considered such an important asset to the community at Durham that it was deemed necessary for an appropriately grand structure to be built in order to house them. Cuthbert was not only a historical figure providing continuity with the community's ancient roots at Lindisfarne, but was also considered a protector of both his community and 'his people'.[29] It was recorded that, after the murder of a Norman earl in 1069, Cuthbert created a dense fog to stop William the Conqueror's forces from finding those guilty.[30] And even William the Conqueror himself had to contend with 'an intolerable heat' caused by Cuthbert when William demanded to see the body of the saint as he was passing through Durham. So distressing was the affliction that he fled the church and the city not stopping until he had crossed the river Tees.[31]

A similar story involves the royal tax collector Ranulf, who became ill attempting to recover taxes from the people of Northumbria, presumably because of Cuthbert's displeasure at his actions, while another account recalls how a Norman soldier attempted to steal some treasure from the church and was later killed by the saint.[32] These stories demonstrate not only the potency of the saint in the late eleventh century but also that even the continental bishops of Durham recognized the importance of using the saint's power in establishing Northumbria's relationship with Norman secular authority.

The first stone of the Cathedral was laid on 11 August 1093 and the entire structure was completed by 1133. It has been compared in its importance and monumental scale to the imperial church at Speyer in Germany and the third abbey church at Cluny in France, two of the most significant buildings of medieval Christendom.[33] The space is monumental with its large decorated piers and elaborate chevron arches and ribbed vaults providing a playful counterpoint to the dark, sober interior.

FIG. 7. Durham Cathedral.

In 1104, Cuthbert's body was placed in a new shrine at the East end of the Cathedral, marking the beginning of a new era for Durham and the cult. At this time the coffin was opened and it was recorded that, to everyone's amazement, the body of the saint was found still to be incorrupt, another affirmation of Cuthbert's power. Two separate accounts of the translation ceremony were made, first by Symeon of Durham, an early-twelfth-century monk of Durham and second in the mid-twelfth century, by the prolific chronicler of Durham's history, Reginald of Durham.[34] In Symeon's account, he records that a small Gospel book in a leather satchel was also found in the inner coffin; this is the Gospel of St John now on loan to The British Library and displayed next to the Lindisfarne Gospels.[35] At the translation ceremony and during his sermon on that occasion, this book, now referred to as the Cuthbert Gospel of St John (and formerly as the Stonyhurst Gospels), was lifted up and displayed to the onlookers by Bishop Flambard (FIG. 8).

FIG. 8. Cuthbert Gospel of St John, exterior binding, on loan to The British Library (by permission of the English Province of the Society of Jesus).

The discovery of this book in the coffin is an example of the importance of the Gospel of John in the Middle Ages and of the practice of using the text as a talisman. In particular, the first words of John, 'In the beginning was the Word, and the Word was with God, and the Word was God', were recited or worn around the neck in the Middle Ages in order to bring health and safety to their owners; even St Augustine believed that John's words could cure headaches.[36] At the discovery of the book in St Cuthbert's coffin, we are told that a monk acquired a silk thread from the satchel's strap and hid it in his shoe. He later became ill and was forced to confess his sin and make restitution to Cuthbert, thereby testifying both to the power of the book and the displeasure of the saint.

In 1153 or 1154, the Archbishop of York, William Fitzherbert, visited Durham Cathedral, presumably at the instigation of his cousin, the new Bishop of Durham, Hugh du Puiset (Bishop 1153–95). While at the high altar the sacristan brought a small book in a leather satchel to William and put it over his head where it hung around his neck from its straps, like a medal. Reginald recounts how William, like Bishop Flambard before him, took the book out of the satchel and displayed it to the onlookers and, paralleling the earlier story, a member of the crowd (this time later that night) handled the manuscript and fell ill.[37] The circumstances of the event must surely have reminded those present of Bishop Flambard's actions fifty years previously. However, there was one significant difference. William did not hold up to the congregation a Gospel of St John, with its powerful opening incantation, but instead held in his hands a *Life of St Cuthbert*. By 1153/54, at the beginning of the episcopacy of Hugh du Puiset, the power to protect and heal had been transferred from the words of John to the biography of their saint, Cuthbert.

During the eleventh and twelfth centuries the interest in relics, saints and pilgrimages was enormous. The suffering and hardship of the pilgrimage, the spectacle and mystery of the gold- and jewel-encrusted reliquary shrines, and the potential healing powers of the saint were irresistible, and provided a unique focus for all people, regardless of class.[38] At the translation of Cuthbert in 1104, Symeon writes that: 'Men of all ranks, ages, and professions, the secular and the spiritual, all hastened to be present'.

Despite their popularity, the cults of the saints had their detractors. Bernard of Clairvaux (1090–1153), one of the most severe critics of Benedictine monastic excess, chastised the pilgrimage trade: 'The eyes are fed with gold-bedecked reliquaries, and the money boxes spring open…People run to kiss it; they are invited to give; and they look more at the beauty than venerate the sacred.'[39]

Although Bernard of Clairvaux's remarks were not addressed specifically to the cult of relics in Durham, they could equally be applied to the situation there. In addition to the incorrupt body of Cuthbert, Durham boasted among its relics the bones of Bede, the head of St Oswald (d.642), a tooth of Queen Margaret of Scotland (d.1093), some hair, a comb and some finger nails from St Malachy, Bishop of Armagh (d.1148), some hair and a rib-bone of Bernard of Clairvaux, the coat of mail, girdle and beard of St Godric of Finchale (d.1170), some hair of St Bartholomew, hermit of Farne who died in 1193, assorted relics of St Nicholas of Bari, a tooth of St William of York, and even some relics of Thomas Becket.

The grand setting for the shrine of Cuthbert's body in Durham Cathedral, along with the other items in its relic collection, no doubt attracted a great many pilgrims in the twelfth century, some having travelled great distances. In addition to pilgrims visiting the shrine of St Cuthbert, Reginald of Durham records that Prior Roger actually encouraged outgoing pilgrims visiting other shrines to bring back marble slabs from their travels in order to adorn the city of Durham. All of this indicates Durham's involvement in the competitive arena of attracting pilgrims, money and gifts for the maintenance and embellishment of the cult of their patron saint.

Thomas Becket and Canterbury

Although the cult of Cuthbert was thriving in the twelfth century the emerging cult of Thomas Becket (*c.*1120–1170) in the 1170s and 1180s, based in Canterbury, challenged the importance and popularity of Durham as a pilgrimage centre.[40] The controversial martrydom of Becket, who was slain within the walls of Canterbury Cathedral by an armed cohort of knights, possibly at King Henry II's inspiration, captured the hearts and imagination of people throughout Europe (FIG. 9). As a result, Becket became the focus of the most important cult in medieval England.

Unlike Cuthbert, Becket was rooted firmly in the secular world. His father was a London merchant who became a clerk of the Archbishop of Canterbury,

FIG. 9. The earliest representation of Thomas Becket's martyrdom, dating from about 1171. British Library, Cotton MS. Claudius B.ii, f.341

Theobald of Bec. It was Theobald who recommended Thomas as Chancellor of England under King Henry II (1154–89). Becket not only became Henry's Chancellor, but also became a close friend. Problems between the two began when Henry wanted to expand royal justice at the expense of the ecclesiastical courts, a move that would have brought the English church under his royal control. Towards this end he appointed Becket Archbishop of Canterbury in 1162, assuming that his friend would act as an ally in his cause and enable him to accomplish his plans without opposition.

However, Becket defended the notion of ecclesiastical independence vigorously, much to the dismay and contempt of Henry, and they became engaged in a heated debate over royal control of the church. This debate led to Henry issuing the *Constitutions of Clarendon*, a document listing a series of royal provisions related to the church, one of which prohibited appeals to Rome without a royal licence, effectively making the crown the arbiter between the church in England and that in Rome.

Central to the debate was whether churchmen, who had been tried in ecclesiastical courts, were then subject to the jurisdiction of the royal courts. According to Henry, these criminals would often be given a 'light' sentence in the ecclesiastical courts, consisting of perhaps being defrocked and then released, even for crimes of murder. In the royal courts such a serious crime warranted the penalty of death or mutilation. The idea of being on trial twice for the same crime incensed Becket who, naturally, argued that such a practice would make a mockery of the ecclesiastical justice system.

Henry then accused Becket of various crimes against the kingdom, leaving Becket little choice but to flee England and seek the support of Pope Alexander III. The Pope did not want to alienate King Henry, but at the same time had to support the cause of Becket. Although a truce was eventually negotiated between Becket and Henry in 1170, many of the issues were still not resolved. This underlying tension became apparent almost immediately upon Becket's return to England when he excommunicated several of Henry's supporters. This act infuriated Henry and inspired four knights of the royal household to go to Canterbury on 29 December 1170 and murder Becket at the high altar.

His death shocked all of Europe and embarrassed Henry. Becket was regarded as a martyr and very swiftly miracles began to be recorded at his tomb, making Canterbury a major pilgrimage centre and the focus of a popular cult. Such was the vigour of the cult, even in its early formation, that Henry was obliged, as an act of penance, to walk through the streets of Canterbury and be flogged by the Canterbury monks.

With the assassination of Thomas Becket and the establishment of his cult in the South, Durham, Cuthbert and the North were once again on the defensive. Durham responded by vigorously promoting Cuthbert and by 'rewriting' his life to include his recent 'miracles', and by creating more splendid architecture, objects and books to glorify him and attract pilgrims. This increased literary and artistic activity surrounding Cuthbert in the 1170s enabled his cult to gain new vigour and popularity.

Hugh du Puiset and Durham

Central to the attempt to reinvigorate the cult and to promote Durham's position in England was Hugh du Puiset, bishop of Durham from 1153–95 and the nephew of Henry of Blois, bishop of Winchester, and King Stephen.[41] He built the elegant Galilee Chapel at the West end of Durham Cathedral, rebuilt the Castle at Durham, built a bridge and a hospital, and commissioned many objects for the Cathedral including a grand candlestick, beautiful vestments studded with pearls and precious stones, and magnificent altar cloths. Upon his death he gave the monastic community over seventy manuscripts, some beautifully illuminated.[42] In short he was a grand bishop.

The Bishops of Durham have often been described as princes, and indeed, Bishop Hugh du Puiset, who was elected unanimously by the Chapter, undoubtedly found himself among the ecclesiastical and princely leaders of Europe when he became head of the great Benedictine foundation at Durham. He was a descendant of the relatively prosperous Le Puiset family from the region around Chartres, who controlled the Paris-Orléans thoroughfare.[43] As William Stubbs has said, he 'was a man whose ancestors had been accustomed to deal on an equality with kings, and to give them no small trouble'.[44]

His desire to stamp his authority on the monastic community resulted in the ill-judged dismissal of Prior Thomas in 1162 which in turn led to friction with the community of monks at Durham.[45] The monks themselves expressed dissatisfaction over Puiset's actions and some of them appear to have written a series of forged charters and documents in the 1160s, 1170s and perhaps even into the 1180s.[46] These documents tend to concern themselves with the rights and privileges of the monastic community in relation to the Bishop, and clearly demonstrate the tension between monk and Bishop during this anxious decade.

Whatever his relationship with the monks might have been, his efforts to revive the cult of Cuthbert cannot be faulted. Hugh du Puiset instigated several ambitious building campaigns during his time as Bishop. He attempted without success to rebuild the eastern end of the cathedral in the early 1170s and was responsible for adding the magnificent Galilee Chapel to the western end of the cathedral. Puiset also had the walls of the Galilee covered with paintings, including images of Cuthbert and Oswald, King of Northumbria (605–42). And finally, although there is no evidence to prove the identity of a patron of the great illuminated London *Life* of St Cuthbert, one should not dismiss Puiset's involvement given the de luxe quality of the manuscript.

Concerning the attempt to enlarge the eastern end of Durham Cathedral, Geoffrey of Coldingham writes that Puiset,

> ...began to construct an aisle at the east end of the church ...[but that]... great cracks appeared in them [the walls] to the peril of the workmen; which was enough to indicate to him that God and his servant Cuthbert disapproved. The work was stopped and transferred to the west, where women would be allowed to enter; so those who had not had access to the secret and holy places might gain solace from the contemplation of them.[47]

The work was transferred to the western end because the eastern building was too difficult to construct, probably as a result of insufficient foundations and because the monks may have been concerned that such a construction would potentially have allowed women access to Cuthbert's shrine, something they would not have entertained. However, the Galilee Chapel, sited at the western end of the cathedral and therefore some distance from Cuthbert's shrine and the liturgical ceremonies, would have allowed women less problematic access to the cathedral. The Galilee Chapel was completed possibly by *c.*1175, but no later than 1189.[48]

A Galilee Chapel, as it was called in an early charter,[49] was placed at the West end of a church where the religious gathered before re-entering the church for Mass, the allusion being Christ's journey from Galilee to Jerusalem prior to his passion. A second function is suggested by court records of the fourteenth century which describe the Bishop's Consistory Court being held in the Galilee. The Chapel was, at least by the fifteenth century, multi-functional: it was a Lady Chapel, it was used as a gathering space for religious functions, and occasionally it was used as an ecclesiastical court-room. Architectural historian Richard Halsey suggests that the combined functions of the building were intended from the beginning. The close proximity of a bishop's court in the Galilee would undoubtedly have reminded the monks of the bishop's power and authority, and would serve to remind them that the chapel itself was the bishop's and not the priory's.

Although Halsey does not speculate on the type of building Puiset was planning at the East end of the Cathedral, he does remark that many of the materials of this earlier structure and probably the form of it were adopted in the Galilee. Halsey further concludes that Puiset wanted to create 'a new and larger setting for the shrine of Cuthbert (which may have involved a translation of the relics), or the creation of an ambulatory with chapels to the east of the shrine'.[50]

Furthermore, the implication of Geoffrey of Coldingham's comment is that the East end was to receive a *plagam*, or aisle, in order to provide a new setting for

28

FIG. 10. The interior of the Galilee Chapel showing the round chevron arches.

the shrine and possibly as an early variant on a Lady Chapel. The planned new shrine at the eastern end would have facilitated greater access to Cuthbert and might have necessitated the re-housing of Cuthbert's relics, both of which would almost certainly have been disconcerting to the monks. However, establishing a larger east end with an ambulatory for the express intention of providing pilgrims with greater access to Cuthbert's shrine makes a great deal of sense when put in the context of a late-twelfth-century revitalization of the cult. Indeed, it was precisely at this time that a new shrine was constructed for Becket at the East end of Canterbury Cathedral as a result of a fire which destroyed the choir.

That this attempt to enlarge the eastern end failed has perhaps more to do with conservative attitudes in the monastery than with the structural problems. Whatever such problems they may have encountered in the late twelfth century, they were overcome by the mid-thirteenth century when the eastern end was successfully expanded with the addition of the Chapel of the Nine Altars.

The Galilee Chapel is perhaps Puiset's best known architectural project simply because it has survived to this day virtually intact, whereas other buildings have not. Given its date of completion, the Galilee is a rather unusual looking structure, and it has inspired a certain amount of debate because of its rather unusual five-aisled plan, its elegant quatrefoil shafts and its position at the western end of the cathedral. Although it adopts certain early gothic forms, its architectural vocabulary is firmly rooted in a northern 'style' and adopts the very ornate chevron decoration and rounded arches found in the Cathedral itself (FIG. 10).[51] This may come as no surprise since it is an annexe to the Cathedral. However, when one considers the building in relation to the new choir at Canterbury Cathedral (begun in 1174) in which the French architect William of Sens was employed and which drew upon and maintained an architectural vocabulary that was considered both 'French' and 'modern' (Gothic), the Galilee looks rather curious, or at least non-French. It can be characterized as very 'Northumbrian' in appearance and, given the relationship between Durham and Canterbury at this time, it may not be too fanciful to suggest that its appearance was intentional and not simply an accidental adoption of common regional building practices.

FIG. 11. The wall-painting of St Cuthbert as bishop in the Galilee Chapel.

There are very few examples of painted images of Cuthbert remaining, but perhaps one of the most telling representations can be found in the south jamb of an arched recess at the East end of the Galilee Chapel, created soon after its completion *c.*1175 (FIG. 11). Although the painted image is thought to represent Cuthbert, there has been some controversy over its identification. Most scholars agree that it depicts Cuthbert, while others have suggested it represents Bishop Puiset.[52] Since Puiset was responsible for the construction of the Galilee Chapel it is reasonable to assume that these contemporary wall paintings were commissioned by him and reflect, to some degree, his interests. The painting stands opposite a painting of a King, thought to be St Oswald, with what was probably a Virgin and Child on the back of the recess.

There is no documentary evidence to suggest an attribution of the figure, therefore, the most we can do is come to a conclusion based on probability. It is likely that the figures represent Cuthbert and Oswald simply because the representation of an ancient King of Northumbria and its patron saint makes sense, especially since the decapitated head of Oswald was placed next to Cuthbert's body in the shrine at the eastern end of the cathedral thereby establishing a pre-existing relationship between the two. It would have been highly unusual to represent the contemporary figures of Puiset and possibly King Richard in such a monumental wall painting during the twelfth century.

The cause of this uncertainty is the way in which the figures are represented, and is itself significant. 'Cuthbert' is depicted as a late-twelfth-century bishop. He is holding a white crozier with a gold band in his left hand; he lifts his right hand in a gesture of blessing. He wears the vestments of the mass with amice, alb, dalmatic, stole, and chasuble, and carries a maniple. His white mitre has ornamented strips of gold and hanging bands. The positioning of the mitre with horns over the front and back, as opposed to the sides, confirms the late twelfth-century date. He is not tonsured, nor does he wear sack-cloth, or humble garb; he is not a monk, nor a prior. He is a twelfth-century bishop. If this is a representation of Cuthbert, then he would have looked remarkably similar to Puiset in his episcopal garb. By depicting Cuthbert in this way Puiset's authority as his legitimate successor would have been reinforced, a fact which Puiset may have been intentionally trying to communicate in such an image.

The depiction of Cuthbert-as-bishop can also be found in the contemporary wall-paintings at the church of St Lawrence, Pittington, several miles from the Cathedral. Because very little remains of this cycle of wall-paintings, it is impossible to draw any overall conclusions about the subject chosen or the reasons certain subjects or stories were selected over others. Even so, it is fortunate, for the purposes of this line of thought, that, of the two remaining scenes, one deals with Cuthbert's consecration as bishop (dealt with by Bede in chapter 24 of the *Life*).[53] Both paintings date from the time of Puiset and further demonstrate the importance of depicting Cuthbert as a bishop to the contemporary Bishop and the monastic community.

As well as the Galilee Chapel, Puiset was involved in other building campaigns which may also be connected to the revitalization of the cult. It has been noted that Puiset was interested in the establishment of a hospital in the Durham area. Although his charitable concerns must be recognized in such an enterprise, one must also take into account that Durham was vying with Canterbury as a pilgrimage centre, and with an increased number of pilgrims came the sick and infirm looking to Cuthbert for a miraculous cure. These people inevitably had to be accommodated, hence the need for more hospitals. The hospital of St Giles, founded by Puiset in *c.*1180 beside the river Kepier, included an infirmary, church, dormitory, hall and court. All of the buildings and staff were generously supplied and paid for by Puiset's endowments.

Reginald of Durham and Cuthbert

Another important figure who attempted to foster the cult in the late twelfth century by 'updating' Cuthbert's accomplishments was Reginald of Durham, Durham's greatest hagiographer after Bede. Besides his biographies of the hermit saint, Godric of Finchale, St Oswald, the seventh-century king of Northumbria, and, most likely, Ebba, the abbess of Coldingham, he wrote *The Little book about the wonderful miracles of Blessed Cuthbert which were performed in recent times* (hereafter called *Libellus*).

Reginald's *Libellus* includes a variety of texts that preface 129 miracle stories which record events from 875 to the third quarter of the twelfth century. It has been demonstrated that there were two stages of writing: the initial 111 chapters (completed before January 1167); the remaining stories (begun no earlier than 1172 and completed in late-1174).[54] Given that Becket was martyred in 1170 it is possible that the second group of stories about Cuthbert was added in response to the increasing fame of the shrine at Canterbury. It is impossible to say in what form these stories were distributed and the extent to which they were available outside the monastic community, but by recording 'new' miracles performed by Cuthbert, Reginald would have encouraged and supported the veneration of Cuthbert by the monastic community and pilgrims. By attracting pilgrims to the shrine he would have been helping to strengthen the economic, social and political position of Durham and the North.

If we compare Reginald's *Libellus* with that of the earlier *Lives* of Cuthbert by Bede and the anonymous author we find that Reginald was concerned to stress the more compassionate and merciful side of Cuthbert's character, to elaborate upon the site of the Cathedral as a place of curative miracles and to soften

32

the misogynistic attitude that was associated with Cuthbert and Durham.

For Reginald, Cuthbert's incorrupt body was an important definer of sanctity. The reported display and witness of the fleshed corpse reaffirmed the sanctity of a dead person and served to encourage the cult of the saint at certain critical moments in the community's history (PLATE 42). Such was also the case with two other great English saints from the South, Etheldreda (d.679) and Edmund (*c*.840–69). The important act of witnessing the body is illustrated in the story of a man who would spend a considerable amount of time cutting the dead Cuthbert's hair and nails, and even talking to Cuthbert on occasion.[55] A similar story can be found in the miracles of St Edmund.[56]

Simple incorruption, however, was often not enough, especially for important patron saints – many saintly corpses were blessed with such a fate. As a result, the patron saint needed something special to set him or her apart. For Cuthbert it was the idea of flexibility, that is, the seeming flexibility of limbs and suppleness of skin, which suggested that Cuthbert was 'fresher' than the other incorrupt saints. Although the idea of the elasticity of Cuthbert's corpse was present in earlier accounts, Reginald takes it upon himself to elaborate upon the theme.[57] He ventures to speculate that the flexibility of Cuthbert was a result of the fluidity of blood, even suggesting that the body of the saint was still, in some mysterious way, breathing after death. Where Etheldreda had an incision in her neck, which had then miraculously healed after her death, and Edmund had had his decapitated head miraculously fused back onto his body, in Durham Cuthbert was almost alive, with flexible joints, flowing blood and gentle breathing. This special quality of Cuthbert's incorrupt corpse made him unique and therefore superior to the saintly corpses in the South.[58]

The vast majority of Reginald's miracle stories about Cuthbert depict him assisting his companions; the most common miracles amongst these are curative. Victoria Tudor, a well-known historian of Durham, points to a significant difference between those miracles recorded before 1170, that is, during the first 111 chapters of the *Libellus*, and those dating from after 1170.[59] The earlier miracles tended to occur in a variety of places, such as the Inner Farne or Lindisfarne, while the majority of the latter miracles took place in and around Durham Cathedral. This was evidently a deliberate attempt on Reginald's part to promote Durham and, in particular, Cuthbert's shrine in Durham Cathedral, as a centre of faith healing to compete with Becket's Canterbury.

Another important aspect of Cuthbert's cult, which was indeed more pronounced in Durham at this time, was the recorded attitude of misogyny. It has been argued that this attitude had less to do with the saint himself than with a desire by the first generations of Benedictine Durham monks to discredit married clergy.[60] Indeed, there are numerous instances in the *Life* which attest to Cuthbert's willingness to engage with women; clearly the misogyny did not originate with the *Life*. The community at Chester-le-Street was comprised of secular clergy and did not engage in strict monastic observance. Hence, one of the liberties practiced by them was marriage, which they continued when they arrived in Durham in 995. This was rebuked by the new Benedictine community at Durham established by William of St Calais in 1083 and it is likely that the misogynistic attitude which came to be associated with Cuthbert originates from this time.

Women were not allowed to enter certain locations, such as Durham Cathedral itself, the cathedral cemetery, and perhaps the conventual church at Lindisfarne.[61] This position must not have endeared the shrine at Durham or, for that matter, Cuthbert's cult to women in general. In the 1170s this presented a problem. The nearby and popular cult of St Godric as well as the saints in the South, such as Becket and Edmund, all boasted a high percentage of women among the pilgrims. Reginald's solution was to include a considerable number of curative miracles in the *Libellus* that involved women within the cathedral area, particularly in the vicinity of the Galilee Chapel.[62]

The completion of the Galilee Chapel at the western end of the Cathedral in *c*.1175 and the introduction of women into this space seems to be symptomatic of the shift in attitudes from the hard-line anti-women sentiment at the turn of the century to a less firm, and more compromising attitude in the late twelfth century. This shift towards a more sympathetic attitude encouraged women into the new annexe (if not into the nave of the church), where they could, with some luck, catch a glimpse of Cuthbert's shrine.[63]

The general trend by hagiographers towards making one's saint look more attractive by softening their 'rough' edges was not unique to Cuthbert.[64] A similar pattern can be found in those saints already mentioned: Etheldreda and Edmund. However, what was curious about Cuthbert was that this process occurred much later than in the cults of other saints. This may indicate a kind of complacency on the part of the Durham monks possibly because of their confidence in Cuthbert as a result of his unchallenged supremacy. It was not until the 1170s and the threat from Becket's cult at Canterbury that it was deemed necessary to employ a more aggressive 'advertising campaign' by publicising the shrine and the Cathedral precinct as a curative centre that did not exclude women.

In one story, Reginald goes one step further and places Cuthbert in a competitive situation with his rival St Thomas. A Norwegian boy whose illness causes him to go to Durham in the hope of being cured by Cuthbert's proximity and power is at the centre of a debate about whether Canterbury (and St Thomas) or Durham (and St Cuthbert) would be the more appropriate place for the boy to go for the most satisfactory results.[65] The boy chooses Durham and is miraculously healed by St Cuthbert. In recording this story, Reginald not only adds another curative miracle to the repertoire of St Cuthbert, but also does so at the expense of St Thomas and by so doing informs the reader of his agenda.

Reginald of Durham and Godric of Finchale

In addition to embellishing Cuthbert's legend, Reginald wrote a *Life* of Godric of Finchale, a local hermit saint. Godric played an important role in events in the late twelfth century and in the attempt to attract pilgrims to the Durham region. In fact, he became the focus of another cult. However, in this case Reginald was creating and promoting a new saint, rather than modernising an existing one.

Although Godric of Finchale was not technically a member of the monastic community of Durham he was appropriated by Durham soon after his death.[66] If Cuthbert was an 'ancient' saint, Godric was his modern equivalent. He happened to die at the right place at the right time, and was therefore very useful for the monastic community at Durham. Godric was a modern hermit, 'a living example of the holy hermit Cuthbert had been'.[67] He was one of several hermits in the area but what ensured his success was his timely death on 21 May 1170,[68] just six months before the martyrdom of Becket. Godric's claims to sanctity were promoted by the monks of Durham, perhaps because they saw in him another candidate to challenge the growing fame of Canterbury.

Godric is said to have died at the impressive age of 105. He lived in a hermitage in Finchale, a short distance north of Durham Cathedral, and was recognized by many as a holy man. His eremetic lifestyle not only reflected that of St Cuthbert himself but also placed him in the context of many other hermit-saints of the Northumbrian and Celtic monastic tradition. It is perhaps no coincidence that it is recorded in his *Life* that he was born in 1065, one year prior to the Norman Conquest. Although this may in fact be his birth date, it seems rather unlikely that a person who lived such an ascetic life would have lived to such a great age, even by today's standards. Why, then, was it necessary for Reginald, his biographer, to place his birth prior to 1066? Perhaps by doing so his intention was to place Godric in a pre-Norman, and therefore more authentically 'Northumbrian' context, thereby bringing him closer to the spiritual roots of Cuthbert and appealing to the vestigial 'indigenous' pre-Norman populace.

The monks of Durham were very concerned that their hermit Godric was not performing any miracles, despite the many being performed by Becket in the South,[69] which suggests they felt a sense of competition between Godric and Becket. This being the case, they did not have to wait long for the first sign of Godric's sanctity. On the vigil of the feast of the birth of St John the Baptist (23 June 1172) Godric performed his first miracle at Finchale, the first of over two hundred miracles subsequently recorded by Reginald.[70] Even at this early stage of the cult there is evidence to suggest that there were many visitors present at this first miracle and, although precise numbers are not available, one can conclude that many local people and possibly others from further afield were thereafter encouraged to visit Finchale.[71]

The birth of St Cuthbert

Another late-twelfth-century text pertaining to St Cuthbert, *On the Birth of St Cuthbert*, may well have been composed at Melrose; it offers the first account of the supposed Irish birth of the saint.[72] It was written by an anonymous author at the same time that Puiset, Reginald and the monastic community were engaged in the promotion of Cuthbert in Durham, therefore it is important to consider the book in this context.

In the preface the author informs the reader of his intentions in writing the book: to collect unrecorded miracles of Cuthbert and present them in a book.[73] Whilst researching these unrecorded miracles and other texts concerned with Cuthbert the author came across 'a certain quarto ... which fell into my hands'. This booklet, he goes on, 'expounded the birth of the Blessed Cuthbert in Ireland, [and] also from what a royal and noble stock he sprang'. The author then describes how Eugenius, bishop of Ardmore, had corroborated Cuthbert's Irish and royal birth.

> Among other things indeed, which he [Eugenius] related about our Cuthbert, a saint from early boyhood, he said that king Muriadach was his father; who by his probity in those days subjugated the kingdom of all Ireland under the sceptre of his monarchical power, and of whose strength and power he had read much in their histories; his mother indeed was called Sabina, who for her religious sanctity and admirable conversation was held in the greatest veneration in her own country, and was reputed among them to be numbered with the elect of God.[74]

Finally, the author describes how, after Cuthbert was brought to England by his mother, she returned to Ireland where she died as a religious in the habit of a holy nun. Although the Irish birth is mentioned, a substantial portion of the preface is dedicated to the careful description of Cuthbert's parents. Here is the strongest evidence for the intention of the author. His point is that Cuthbert's pedigree is, therefore, of the highest order in both the ecclesiastical and secular spheres confirming both his princely and saintly status.

It is perhaps no coincidence that Cuthbert's more worldly pedigree was elaborated upon by this author, at a time when Becket posed a threat to Cuthbert's primacy. In so doing, Cuthbert was described as more than a simple hermit saint, rather as someone with princely connections who was clearly part of the aristocratic culture of Ireland and Northumbria. Becket may have been the son of a London merchant, but Cuthbert was the son of a King.

It is virtually impossible to tell precisely how Becket's cult had an impact upon that of Cuthbert's. There are no statistical records for the number of pilgrims attending the shrine in Durham, few indications of the number of local as opposed to 'foreign' people in attendance, and no record of the smaller gifts bestowed upon Cuthbert and the shrine by the average pilgrim and how the quantity of gifts were affected by Becket's cult. The evidence which suggests a perceived threat to Durham by the cult of Becket is limited but important and resides in the subtle anxieties of the monks expressed when comparing the lack of miracles performed by Godric in relation to the great number performed by Becket. The evidence also resides in the important comparisons made by Reginald in the *Libellus* between Cuthbert and Becket. Further circumstantial evidence can be found in the attempts to renew the fabric of Cuthbert's shrine, the construction of the Galilee Chapel, the establishment of a hospital for the sick and infirm, and the production of a lavish *Life of Cuthbert*. This frenzy of architectural and artistic production in the 1170s and 1180s all centred upon Durham and Cuthbert and occur at precisely the same time that Becket was being 'promoted' in the South.

Chapter 3

The *Life* of St Cuthbert

(BL Yates Thompson MS 26)

The manuscript in the British Library, known as Yates Thompson MS 26 (also known as Add MS 39943) was produced in Durham in the late twelfth century during the time when the cult of Cuthbert was being actively promoted by the community of monks and Bishop Puiset.[75] Like the Lindisfarne Gospels and the great cathedral at Durham, this beautifully illuminated manuscript was made in order to honour saint Cuthbert. And like the book that William Fitzherbert held on the high altar in the mid-twelfth century, this manuscript must have had a similar stature and power for both the owner and the beholders. Because it is one of the most extensively illustrated saint's *Lives*, it provides important material for the study of hagiography in general, and allows a critical glimpse into the process of cult rejuvenation at Durham during the Middle Ages.

History of the manuscript

The manuscript was acquired by The British Library in 1920 as part of the collection of Yates Thompson and is considered to be one of the great treasures of the Library's medieval holdings. Despite its importance and the regard in which it is held, its past remains a partial mystery. It can confidently be identified as the manuscript referred to in the 1391 and 1416 catalogues of Durham Cathedral. These catalogues record the first word of the second folio of the manuscript (the 'secundo folio'), a common practice in the Middle Ages used to determine specific manuscripts, all of which were hand-written and therefore would have slightly different words on the second folios of copies of the same text. Hence the reference *ii. fo. dubiorum* in the medieval catalogues proves this to be the book in question as *dubiorum* is, indeed, the first word on the second leaf.[76] Furthermore, analysis of the text by Bertram Colgrave, former Reader in English at the University of Durham, has pointed to a Durham origin for the manuscript.[77]

Next to the entry for this book in the 1416 catalogue is written 'Ricardus Archiepiscopus Eboracensis'. This probably indicates that it was borrowed at some time by Richard le Scrope, the Archbishop of York who was killed in 1405.

It has been suggested that the Bishop may have borrowed the book on behalf of Thomas Langley, dean from 1401–5, and who, while bishop of Durham (1406–37), donated money for the erection of the St Cuthbert window at York Cathedral.

A connection can also be made between this manuscript and Carlisle Cathedral, where it seems that an artist copied seventeen of the scenes from Yates Thompson MS 26 on the backs of the choir stalls. Richard Bell, Bishop of Carlisle, may provide the link as he was the prior at Durham between 1464–78 and the paintings themselves date to the late-fifteenth century.

The whereabouts of the manuscript is unknown from the late fifteenth to the eighteenth century when Thomas Rudd, librarian at Durham Chapter Library from 1717–26, referred to specific textual variations of a *Life of Cuthbert* then owned by Johannis Forcer. Colgrave has checked these variant readings with the British Library manuscript and has concluded that Forcer did indeed once own Yates Thompson MS 26. The ownership of the manuscript seems to have been transferred to Sir Henry Lawson of Brough by 1828 when James Raine referred to it in his book entitled *St Cuthbert*. Both the Lawsons of Brough and the Forcers were well-known Roman Catholic families in the North throughout the eighteenth century and can be linked by Isabelle Lawson who was the maternal grandmother of John Forcer. It is not surprising that such a wonderful relic of the past should have been so carefully preserved by these families.

It was Sir John Lawson who sold the book at Sotheby's in 1906 to the famous manuscript collector Henry Yates Thompson and, after his demise, through the good offices of his wife, it finally found its resting place in The British Library.

Evidence for dating the manuscript

In trying to determine the date of the manuscript one must consider both the palaeography and the decoration. The scribal hand fits very neatly into the late twelfth century. It displays none of the characteristics of an early-thirteenth-century hand, such as the more upright letter-forms and distinctive angular aspect of the hand.[78] In this sense it is not consistent with turn-of-the-century scribal habits found in Durham and elsewhere. Although very homogenous, it has affinities with manuscripts such as the Puiset Bible dating from the early 1170s (DCL MS A.II.1), and to a greater degree a Glossed Pauline Epistle from Durham dating to the 1180s (DCL MS A.II.19) (FIG. 12).

The decoration is comprised of a series of framed, panelled miniatures and two decorated initials. The closest specific stylistic parallel occurs between the standing figure of St Cuthbert on the Frontispiece (PLATE 1) and the painted figure of Cuthbert in the Galilee Chapel which has been variously dated, but

must have been completed no later than *c.*1185 (FIG. 11). T.S.R. Boase, a promi-
nent art historian, has compared the prefatory miniature to the seal of Prior
Bertram (1189–1212).[79] The style of many of the figures, their drapery and the
manner of the execution of the heads, can be compared to the figure style of the
Copenhagen Psalter (Copenhagen, Royal Library MS Thott. 143 2°), also a northern English product of the third quarter of the twelfth century, and the Leiden
Psalter (Leiden, University Library, MS Lat. 76A), of a slightly later date. Art
historian Malcolm Baker characterized the figure style as 'a well developed
transitional style in which Byzantine elements seem well absorbed'.[80] Otto Pächt
and Jonathan Alexander, both medieval manuscript specialists, suggested that the
artist of the London *Life* was also responsible for the initials in a copy of the
Sermons of Maurice de Sully (Oxford, Bodleian Library, Douce MS 270) dating
from the late twelfth century.[81]

The decorated initials 'D' (fol. 2v) and 'P' (fol. 9) (PLATE 3) have typically
late-twelfth-century Durham panelled backgrounds and intertwined scroll
vegetation and are similar to decorated initials found in other Durham manuscripts
such as the Glossed Pauline Epistle previously mentioned (DCL MSS A.II.19)
(FIG. 12) and another *Life of Cuthbert* (B.IV.35). The
use of panelled frames suggests a date later than
the early 1170s, when they began to be introduced
as a decorative feature to the Puiset Bible, possibly
in imitation of glossed books from Paris which
were becoming available in Durham in the 1170s
and 1180s.[82]

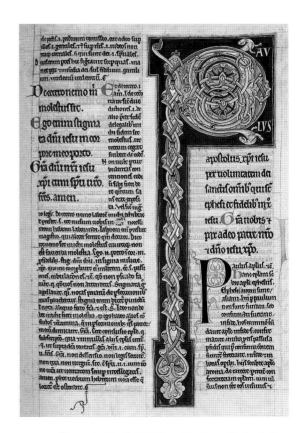

Although it is difficult to date the manuscript
precisely, especially since the evidence is based
upon placing the style of the illuminations within
a stylistic chronology that is necessarily incom-
plete, the manuscript does seem to fit most
comfortably in the 1180s. Any later and the conservative hand would not make sense; any earlier
and the figure style would be inconsistent with that
found in other Durham manuscripts.

The structure of the manuscript

Analysis of the physical structure of the book
enables historians to understand better the
manner in which it was produced and, to a certain
extent, its subsequent history. The way in which a

FIG. 12. Decorated initial 'P' from Durham Cathedral
Library MS A.II.19, 199v.

book is physically constructed varies over time and even from region to region. However, all medieval manuscripts were constructed by sewing together 'gatherings' or 'quires'. A gathering is comprised of a certain number of 'leaves' made from parchment. Once a gathering was written and sometimes illuminated these 'booklets' were then sewn together and possibly bound to form a manuscript.

Yates Thompson MS 26 is comprised of fifteen gatherings, not all of which were made from a consistent number of leaves (see Appendix). The prefatory epistles and Bede's prose *Life*, plus the usual two miracle stories taken from Bede's *Ecclesiastical History*, span the first eight gatherings, which adopt a consistent twelve leaves. Additional texts such as Symeon's *History of the translation of Cuthbert*, and certain other extracts from Symeon (which were not decorated) extend over the remaining seven gatherings. These gatherings do not have a uniform number of leaves.

The question this raises, therefore, is whether the manuscript was originally conceived in its present form or whether the additional textual material (quires 9–15) were written or added to the *Life* at a later date. The break in the quire structures at the ninth gathering would also suggest a slightly different campaign of writing, which may have involved a different scribe and/or the use of a different exemplar.

However, there is also evidence to indicate that the manuscript was written as a coherent entity. First of all, the hand is very consistent. Although at least two scribes were involved in producing the manuscript the overall look is very homogenous, suggesting that an attempt had been made on the part of the scribes to maintain uniformity of script throughout.[83] Furthermore, there is no obvious scribal change between the first part of the manuscript, containing Bede's *Life*, and the second part, containing the additional material. Although the gatherings become more inconsistent in terms of the number of leaves after quire 9, the page rulings and text space are uniform and consistent. All of this would suggest that the manuscript was constructed either from the outset as a coherent entity or was brought together or supplemented early in its existence in its present form. As the additional textual material is concerned with Cuthbert and the cult, it would therefore have made sense to include it with the text of his *Life*.

Picturing the Life of Cuthbert

The survival of an illuminated saint's *Life* is extremely rare, let alone one that has such a large number of high-quality pictures. This section will consider the narrative components and techniques employed in illustrating the *Life of Cuthbert*.[84] It will demonstrate the implications and importance of editing a visual image and how an artist or patron could subtly change meaning by editing the manner in which the saint or events were portrayed. Essential to this section is a comparison with Oxford University College MS 165, the early-twelfth-century *Life of Cuthbert*.[85] Similarities and differences will be addressed, in particular the desire on the part of the Yates Thompson 26 artist to portray Cuthbert in a more humane and sympathetic manner. The implications of such a characterization will be explored in relation to the fostering of the cult.

Yates Thompson MS 26 has forty-six surviving pictures out of an original fifty-five. The artist who painted these elaborate and beautiful miniatures is not named. Although many artists' and scribes' names are known from the twelfth century, it is by no means the norm to find artists' 'signatures'. Although the manuscript itself is quite small, the pictures, with one exception, are full-page framed illuminations. Some are presented as a pair over a double-page opening, but the majority are single scenes set at the beginning of each section of text. The inclusion of full-page miniatures to illustrate Cuthbert's life is very different from the approach taken in the earlier Oxford *Life of Cuthbert*, where scenes were placed between chapters, similar to the manner in which they are placed in the Utrecht Psalter (Utrecht, University Library, Ms. 32, *c*.835). The Oxford *Life* is significant because it is the first attempt in England at elaborate narrative illustration to have been undertaken after the Norman Conquest. It is very likely that it was also made in Durham and would have been, therefore, the logical exemplar for the Yates Thompson manuscript. Its style is still in keeping with the earlier Anglo-Saxon manner of monochrome outline drawings, but in its attempt to depict the narrative of the text it is unprecedented in an English context.

The primary difference between the approach taken in the Oxford *Life* and the London *Life* was discussed by Otto Pächt in his provocative book on pictorial narrative published in 1962.[86] The difference can be summarized as follows: the pictures in the Oxford *Life* combine two separate incidents of a story into one scene, often depicting an action immediately prior to and after a miraculous event. By bringing together the separate events, Pächt suggests that a sense of time is introduced into the narrative and Cuthbert is visually and compositionally denoted as the cause of the miracle in question. In terms of hagiographical illustration a comparison can be made to the *Life of St Benedict and St Maur* from Monte Cassino now housed in the Vatican Library (Biblioteca Apostolica Vaticana, cod. lat. 1202).[87]

For the most part, this desire to combine two incidents into one scene does not occur in the London *Life*. Instead, when two linked events are depicted they are placed on separate facing pages, simplified and framed, thereby visually reinforcing their individuality. The miniatures have multiple frames and panel backgrounds, which also tends to give an iconic appearance and feel to the pictures. Events are simplified, and where there are groups of figures depicted they tend to occupy a separate space to that of Cuthbert. Cuthbert is usually represented at some distance from others, and often placed centrally (PLATES 11, 33).

Although land and sea are represented by simple bands of colour, the representation of geography is not a primary concern (PLATES 12, 13). Pictorial architecture plays a limited role, but is most in evidence in the representation of buildings at Lindisfarne and the hermitage on Farne (PLATES 20–24).

What is perhaps most noticeable about the miniatures is the elaborate use of colour and the large amount of gold used in the panel backgrounds. This is especially apparent if one compares it to the earlier Oxford *Life* with its muted washes and outline drawing style. It was as if the makers of the London *Life* wanted to make a beautifully rich, coloured version of the Oxford *Life*. This desire to produce a colourful version of an earlier monochromatic exemplar can be paralleled in the latest copy of the Utrecht Psalter (Paris, Bibliothèque Nationale, MS. Lat. 8846) in which a great deal of colour was applied. William Noel, an important scholar of medieval manuscripts, has suggested that the makers of this manuscript must have regarded the Utrecht Psalter as unfinished, given its monochrome character, and that the 'Paris' artists considered their job to be to create a new, up-to-date and colourful version of the Psalm text.[88] Whatever the intention of the makers of the London *Life* may have been, the result was the same: a new, up-to-date and splendidly colourful *Life* of Cuthbert was accomplished.

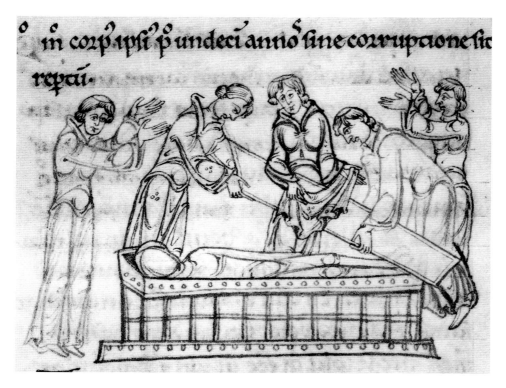

FIG. 13. Discovery of Cuthbert's incorrupt body. *Life* of St Cuthbert, Oxford, University College MS 165, p. 118.

Each chapter received an illustration that was placed after the chapter heading and before the text. However, Chapters 3, 7, 11, and 34 received two illustrations and Chapter 24 received three (PLATES 27–29), the reasons for which remain unclear. It is probable that Chapter 4 received two illustrations although they were excised at some point in the past. The fact that Chapters 3, (4), 7, 11, 24 and 34 received more than one illustration might suggest that they were somehow considered either more complex narratives, which therefore required more visual illustration, or they were thought to be more important than other chapters and therefore warranted an additional scene. A third possibility might be that the artist was responding to the theme described in the chapter heading. Typically the chapter heading, or capitula, was placed on the previous page to the illustration, therefore, the chapter heading would have been read by the artist and may have functioned as an *aide-mémoire* or prompt for the content of the illustration. However, even though this may have been the case with Chapters 3, 7, 11, and 34 (all of which have rather more complicated chapter headings), it does not justify the additional scene in Chapter 24 nor the lack of an additional scene in other chapters in which the chapter headings describe an equally complicated set of events (especially, for example, Chapter 8 in which Cuthbert was healed of sickness and then Boisil prophesied things in Cuthbert's future career) (PLATE 10).

There are two additional miniatures that preface the *Life* and form a double-page spread. First, an image of a monk at the feet of St Cuthbert (PLATE 1). Second, a tonsured, seated scribe writing in a codex (PLATE 2) which is thought to depict Bede writing the *Life of Cuthbert*. To include an author portrait at the beginning of the book was not an uncommon practice in de luxe manuscripts during the Middle Ages. In addition, by the twelfth century there are also examples of portraits of the scribes who had written the particular manuscript, the most famous English example being the scribe Eadwine from the Eadwine Psalter (Cambridge, Trinity College, MS. R.17.1, folio 283v, *c.*1160–70).[89] In Durham, an example of a scribal portrait occurs in a copy of St Augustine's (354–430) commentary on the Psalms in which the scribe 'Robert' is represented (DCL Ms B.II.13, fol. 102).[90]

Cuthbert digging with a monk. Detail from Plate 21. BL Yates Thompson MS 26, f.41.

It is uncertain as to whether Chapter 1 once had an image; the text begins with a decorated initial 'P', and since no other chapter begins with such an elaborately decorated initial, it would tend to indicate that a miniature was not planned for the chapter. The image prefacing Chapter 2 has been excised.[91] The opening pair of scenes depicting Cuthbert and Bede is echoed in its composition in Chapter 3 on folios 10v and 11 with a double-page spread representing the boy Cuthbert praying (PLATES 4 and 5). He does so in order to calm the tumultuous sea and to recover the rafts, images which illustrate Chapter 3. In order to accentuate the uncontrollable sea the artist has broken convention by depicting the sea running freely over the frame of the image and onto the opposite page. The effect is both to isolate Cuthbert on the left-hand side while linking him with his colleagues on the right-hand side. The calming of the storm has resonances of the miracle performed by Christ and immediately presents the viewer with a parallel between Christ and the Saint.

The miracle of the loaves and fishes performed by Christ is also loosely mirrored by a series of miracles from Chapters 5, 7, 11 and 12 all of which concern themselves with finding bread or fish in an unusual way (PLATES 6, 8, 9 and 13–15). The close relationship between Christ and Saint should not be surprising given that Pope Gregory's notion of *Imitatio Christi*, as described in chapter 1, was central to hagiographical writing.

It is also important to consider the subtle differences between the way in which Cuthbert was represented in this manuscript and the earlier Oxford *Life*, which would have provided an obvious exemplar to the Durham artist and patron. By comparing the two, a clearer understanding of the intentions of the artist or patron in making such a sumptuously illustrated book become clear.

For instance, in Chapter 6 Cuthbert is received into the monastery at Melrose (PLATE 7). This may seem like a reasonably straightforward event, but a comparison between the illustrations of this event in the London and Oxford manuscripts betrays subtle changes. In the Oxford *Life* Cuthbert is greeted by Boisil at the entrance from a short distance (FIG. 14). By contrast, in the London *Life*, he is embraced by Boisil on the threshold of the monastery. This gesture of friendship could not have escaped the notice of the late-twelfth-century community at Durham who would have been aware of, or involved with, a renewed interest in the discourse and idea of friendship from former members of their own community like Ailred of Rievaulx and Prior Lawrence.[92] One might even speculate that the iconography of the scene might have been informed by such contemporary concerns.

In addition, by depicting Cuthbert in this way his more humane and vulnerable side is being represented, in keeping with the attempts by Reginald to make him a more sympathetic character. An image like this would have reinforced Reginald's efforts and, therefore, further helped to promote the cult.

FIG. 14. Cuthbert greeted by Boisil at Melrose Abbey. *Life* of St Cuthbert, Oxford, University College MS 165, p. 23

Cuthbert's time with Boisil at Melrose is also illustrated in the scene prefacing Chapter 8, in which Cuthbert and Boisil are engaged in earnest conversation (PLATE 10). Boisil, on his deathbed, spent a week with Cuthbert imparting his knowledge to him, and as part of this week-long conversation Boisil asked Cuthbert to read St John's Gospel. However, it was not just any manuscript of the text but one which he had in his possession that was seven quires long. He asked Cuthbert to read one quire per day. This is unusual for various reasons, not least because it is a remarkably rare medieval reference to the physical collation of a manuscript.

The fact that it was St John's Gospel that Cuthbert was reading and that the manuscript in question was comprised of seven gatherings did not go unnoticed by the community of monks at Durham. Therefore, when the coffin was opened at the translation ceremony in 1104 and a Gospel of St John was found inside, it was natural that the monks jumped to the conclusion that this was Boisil's book – despite the manuscript, the Cuthbert Gospel of St John, being twelve quires long. This was the manuscript that Bishop Flambard displayed to those present at his sermon (FIG. 8).

It was widely believed that the first verses of St John's Gospel had apotropaic powers; there is a story (possibly apocryphal) told by John of Salisbury that Cuthbert himself cured a sick man by the placing the gospel upon him.[93] Church authorities, such as the renowned scholar Alcuin (*c*.735–804), condemned the practice of wearing relics, such as saints' bones and texts of the Gospel, but this did not lessen popular belief in the miraculous powers of these items.[94] It is significant that in Reginald's recollection of the events surrounding William Fitzherbert's visit to Durham in 1153 or 1154, a manuscript of Cuthbert's *Life* was used in a similar manner and was therefore also attributed such appeal and power.

Even though the Cuthbert Gospel of St John in The British Library was clearly not Boisil's book, the fact that it was read by Boisil at the end of his life and the fact that a Gospel of John was found in Cuthbert's coffin suggest that it had a special meaning for Boisil and Cuthbert and conforms to what is known about the use of the Gospel text in the Middle Ages. The depiction of Boisil and Cuthbert's conversation in the *Life* may have prompted the reader to recall the famous events of the translation and William Fitzherbert's associated act.

Cuthbert making his hermitage with the help of an angel.
Detail from Plate 20. BL Yates Thompson MS 26, f.39.

The miniatures illustrating the making of Cuthbert's hermitage on Farne are fascinating for several reasons (PLATES 20–24). First, it is recalled in the *Life* that no one had been able to inhabit the remote island of Farne before because of the terrible phantoms of demons which dwelt there. Cuthbert, therefore, had to rid the place of these demons once he arrived and this he does in Chapters 13 and 17. In PLATE 20 he is shown gesturing towards the upper right-hand corner of the picture where a hideous beast is depicted outside the frame of the miniature escaping from the page. Here, once again, the artist chooses to break the frame in order to make a more effective image – the use of the frame here denotes the sacred space of Farne and the artist uses it to illustrate the fact that the demons no longer dwell there.

Second, the depiction of the structure that he builds is far grander than that described in the text. In fact, it expressly contradicts the text. The text recounts how the building was cut out of the living rock and was constructed where necessary with rough stone and turf with the aid of an angel. In other words it would have looked like a cave. In the depiction we see that an angel is helping Cuthbert to make a circular-planned building with finely cut stone and mortared walls. Furthermore, in this image the two events of him driving away the demons and being assisted by the angel are incorporated into a single scene similar to the practice of integrating events in the earlier Oxford *Life*.

The sturdy, well-constructed hermitage plays a central role in the illustrations of the next few chapters. First of all, Cuthbert finds a well nearby (PLATE 21), then expels birds from the land whilst standing at the doorstep of the hermitage (PLATE 22). Next, the birds pick at the thatched roof of the structure (PLATE 23), and finally he discovers a timber roof-beam of the correct length for the hermitage washed up on the beach (PLATE 24). Clearly the late-twelfth-century artist was somewhat taken by the physical structure of the hermitage and the role it played in Cuthbert's life. As was the custom at the time, he chose to represent the way he knew such a structure might have looked, rather than what the text described, leaving us with an image of a contemporary building.

Chapters 29–33 inclusive are concerned with a series of curative miracles performed by Cuthbert (PLATES 33–35). The image for Chapter 32 has, unfortunately, been excised. In the remaining pictures in this series, there are two images which deserve more comment and which visually elaborate upon the theme of Cuthbert's iconic status and upon his caring, more humane character.

In Chapter 31 Bede recounts how Cuthbert blessed some bread that was later used to cure a sick man (PLATE 34). He clearly separates the episodes of the blessing of the bread and the curative miracle. In fact, he begins by saying that the miracle was performed despite Cuthbert's absence. In other words the whole point of the story is to illustrate Cuthbert's powers to heal and the fact that he could perform a healing miracle through some other agent or object. His physical presence was not necessary.

However, the artist chose to represent the scene in a different way. He chose to depict Cuthbert himself giving the sick man the bread. One might argue that this undermines the whole point of Bede's story – by depicting Cuthbert actually giving the man the bread, the notion that Cuthbert can cure by proxy is lost. However, the artist realized that if he depicted someone else administering to the sick, he would be faced with the dilemma that it would look as if the miracle was performed not by Cuthbert, but by an intermediary figure.

Chapter 33 continues the emphasis on the power of Cuthbert by recounting the healing of a dying boy (PLATE 35). Although Cuthbert is physically separate from the mother and her child the proximity between the figures suggests a certain intimacy which reflects Reginald's concern to make Cuthbert a more appealing character, especially to women. Here, the depiction of the intermediary figure of the child being held out towards Cuthbert acts a bridge between the two and alludes to a paternal and sympathetic aspect of his character. Granted, the story itself is from Bede's text, but by depicting this aspect of the story, the artist chose to bring to the viewer's attention this intimate moment between Cuthbert, child and mother.

An intriguing pair of scenes illustrates Chapter 34 (PLATES 36 and 37). The two images form a double-page spread between folios 63v and 64. The image of a man falling from a tree is unique in its size and in the fact that it has a patterned red background, quite dissimilar to the other miniatures in this manuscript, all of which have a panel of gold with some other colour panelling, usually red or blue. On the facing page is an image of Cuthbert and two other figures at a table. According to the text, Cuthbert has just dropped his knife and is in a trance. The woman is asking him or is about to ask him what he is seeing in his vision.

In this image we can clearly see the way in which the artist was trying to show the relationship between Cuthbert and his vision. He does so by placing him next to the adjacent page and has Cuthbert gesture towards the previous page as he lays down the knife and gazes towards the falling figure. The depiction of the vision is smaller than the usual miniatures thereby setting off its uniqueness; the artist chose to further signal the visionary aspect of the event by incorporating a patterned background. The size of the picture and the background are visual clues to the scene's meaning and signify that it is part of Cuthbert's vision, and not simply a depiction of an event. In this respect, the image shares in a slightly later tradition of the thirteenth century of using background panels and colours to denote a picture's special or peculiar character.[95]

This attention to visual detail in the *Life* suggests that Durham illuminators and illustrators were very conscious of the role visual imagery could play in elucidating and even commenting upon the text. Images were not simply illustrations but provided an arena for developing thought-provoking and meaningful visual/textual dialogues.

The closing episodes in the *Life* were important ones to illustrate because they depict the important moment of Cuthbert's death (PLATE 40) as well as the posthumous miracles and the discovery of his incorrupt body. The picture of his death emphasizes the relinquishing of his spirit to God. He looks towards Christ and the angels who are ready to receive his spirit. The event mirrors the text in its depiction of Cuthbert raising his hand in the company of his monks at the moment of death.

Just before his death Cuthbert urges the monks to: 'Always keep peace and divine charity amongst yourselves; and when necessity compels you to take council about your affairs, see to it most earnestly that you are unanimous in your councils.'

Although the accompanying illustration represents the actual moment of his death, the image must have triggered Cuthbert's last words in the mind of the viewer. In particular, the reference to unanimity must have struck a chord with the reader in view of the controversy surrounding the dismissal of Prior Thomas. In addition, it would have reminded the community not only of their own unanimous election of Cuthbert as bishop in the late seventh century, but also of their more recent unanimous election of Bishop Puiset in 1153. In this way, the image serves to remind the viewer of both events and of Cuthbert's last words – words that would have had a particular relevance for the late-twelfth-century community.

Medieval pictures were never simply copies. Although the expressions 'innovation' and 'creativity' are not perhaps associated with medieval art, the inventive and the creative are there, embedded in the 'traditional', for those who care to look. Artists and patrons were concerned with making up-to-date images and part of the process meant making more colourful versions of earlier pictures, editing and changing their content, and elaborating upon the gestures of those depicted or upon the clothing they wore. All of these innovations were important and necessary to the makers and provide historians with a glimpse into the creative processes and the 'hidden' agendas of both patrons and artists.

It was a concern of the monastic community at Durham that Cuthbert be represented in a more likeable manner and, therefore, the imagery conforms to their own view of Cuthbert. However, is there any evidence to suggest a specific patron?

It has been suggested that the London *Life* was written and illustrated in the community for its own use.[96] But, unfortunately, there is absolutely no proof that the manuscript was made for either the monastic community in general or for a particular individual either within or without that community. The evidence of its later ownership by the monastic community does not necessarily mean that it was made by an individual monk or a collective group. Nor does it necessarily mean that the illuminations must be understood in terms of 'their interest and relevance to the monastic community'.[97]

However, the picture cycle in the London *Life* is extensive and the production of such an elaborate manuscript would have been a major undertaking. There were over fifty scenes illustrating the manuscript, incorporating extensive use of coloured pigments and gold backgrounds. If the illustrations represent the attitude of the Durham episcopate rather than the monastic community, it is very likely that Puiset was involved with its production.

In trying to determine a possible patron two scenes from the London *Life* must be considered. These two pictures are not present in the earlier Oxford *Life*. They are the Frontispiece (PLATE 1) and the scene of St Cuthbert being chosen at the synod by monks (Chapter 24, PLATE 29). Since these images were introduced either by the illuminator or at the request of the patron they must reflect the artist's and/or patron's concerns. Furthermore, there is one significant picture that is present in the Oxford *Life*, but omitted from the London *Life*: that of Cuthbert washing the monks' feet from Chapter 18.

Chapter 24 is the only chapter to be illustrated by three scenes. The first two scenes are placed in the 'normal' way, that is, prefacing the text (PLATES 27, 28).

FIG. 15. The monks of Christ Church before St Benedict. British Library MS Arundel 155, f.133.

However, the picture of Cuthbert at the synod is placed after the chapter heading for Chapter 25 and before its first illumination. In other words, this placing suggests that the image is something of an after-thought, or at least it was not planned in the 'original' scheme of things. If it was intended originally, it would surely have been placed following the pictures to Chapter 24 and not crammed in between Chapters 24 and 25. This tends to corroborate the unusual aspect of this picture and further raises the question of its inclusion.

Chapter 24 deals entirely with Cuthbert's acceptance of the bishopric, and this additional picture represents the unanimous consent of the monks to have

Cuthbert as their bishop. It does not, as has been argued, refer to Cuthbert's acceptance of the role of prior.[98] The right to freely elect the bishop was a problem in the early to mid-twelfth century. The appointments were riddled with nepotism, especially in England and this was cause for increasing concern on the part of monastic communities – so much so that a Papal Bull was issued by Pope Urban III in 1186 which stated that the bishop should be elected by the common consent of the monks. The image in this manuscript, written and illuminated at precisely this date, has resonances of this decree, and serves to demonstrate that Cuthbert's authority was enhanced by his free election to his position.

Like Cuthbert, Bishop Hugh du Puiset was elected unanimously by the monastic congregation – he was even likened to David by Prior Lawrence because, despite his tender years, he was a wise person. That such a picture, highlighting Cuthbert's election and popular support, should have been included, must surely have been with the aim of reminding the reader of Puiset's free election to bishop. At a time of great tension between Puiset and the monks, arising from Puiset's dismissal of Prior Thomas in the early 1160s, an image like this must have been intended to reinforce his position as rightful successor to Cuthbert and as the legitimate authority in Durham.

The second significant image is that of the Frontispiece (PLATE 1) where a prostrate monk adores Cuthbert. Cuthbert is depicted as bishop in a very similar manner to his representation in the Galilee wall painting. In fact, in many respects, the images are almost identical.[99] Furthermore, the monk is shown prostrate, reaching out and grasping the right foot of the bishop and kissing it.

In the pictorial tradition the iconography of 'proskynesis' is linked with the cross, or the crucifixion. It probably originated in Early Christian art. There remain, for instance, some sixth-century pilgrim flasks that show pilgrims kneeling before and touching the crucified Christ. The scriptural source is Philippians 2:3–11 in which the faithful are encouraged to adore the cross with bended knee. This was taken as the explanation of the way in which the cross was venerated in the Good Friday liturgy by a Carolingian liturgist, Amalarius of Metz (c.775–c.850). He said that while kneeling before the cross the worshipper imagined Christ upon it and therefore his posture before the cross emulated Christ's humility.

This act was represented numerous times, perhaps most famously in the image of Hrabanus Maurus kneeling before the Cross which begins his famous book *De laudibus sanctae crucis*, a book which was often copied during the Middle Ages (for instance, Cambridge, Trinity College MS. B.16.3). In this image, however, we find a monk kneeling before Cuthbert – neither emperor, nor Christ. His habit and tonsure identify him as Benedictine. There is no inscription indicating his role, if any, in the book's production as there might have been if this image was depicting the artist or patron. He does not hold a pen nor does he hold an image of a book as a donor might.

There are more immediate iconographic precedents. For example, in a tenth-century Rule of St Benedict (BL Arundel MS 155), a monk named Eadui Basan, prostrates himself humbly before St Benedict (FIG. 15).[100] Next to Benedict are the donors, a large throng of monks offering St Benedict a codex upon which are written the opening words of the Prologue to the Rule: 'Listen, my son, to the precepts...'. The prostrate monk wears a belt or girdle upon which is written 'zona humilitatis'; the theme of humility runs throughout the Rule.

The act of prostration crops up several times in the Rule (Chapters 44, 53, 58, 67, 71).[101] It may be useful to see in what context monks were required to prostrate themselves in their daily life.[102] After all, images such as these are not simply informed by visual associations of an iconographic type but must surely have associations with daily monastic customs. It is difficult to assess whether such an image would have had any or all of the associations that proskynesis had for a monk. One might assume that this posture was simply one of humility, but in the Rule, at least, it was used in certain situations associated with punishment and chastisement.

However, in this image of Cuthbert and the monk there is a further gesture: the kiss. It would be useful if this were a Judas-kiss, and, therefore, an image of a monk betraying a bishop; however, it is not a kiss on the cheek, but a kiss on his foot, an act that even today is one of submission and humility. There is no precedent for the representation of a monk kissing the feet of a saint, or bishop. In the representation of Benedict and the prostrate monk from Arundel 155, the monk does come perilously close to puckering his lips at the foot of Benedict, but he stops short, leaving his lips taut and simply brushing his cheek on the foot instead.

The kiss does play a part in the Good Friday liturgy. Lanfranc's monastic constitutions tell us that on Good Friday the abbot and the vested ministers shall approach the cross, prostrate themselves and then each one should kiss the feet of the crucifix before returning to the choir. This particular text was known in Durham in the twelfth century; in fact the monastic community possessed a copy of it (DCL MS B.IV.24).[103] The other instance of such an act takes place on the previous day when the feet and hands of the poor were washed by the brethren and then kissed.

Given the gestures of the figures, this image is, therefore, more complex than one might have initially assumed. It is a scene in which the monk adores, is submissive towards, or venerates the saint, in this case St Cuthbert-as-bishop. In addition, it has resonances of the liturgical prostration and kissing of the cross or crucifixion as experienced by contemporary worshippers. Even though the image is quite clearly of Cuthbert, the gesture of the monk towards Cuthbert is that reserved for Christ and the Cross on Good Friday.

The gestural associations charge the image with added meaning. Cuthbert not only assumes icon-like status because of the gold background, but also has

Christ-like status because of the monk's gesture. This is not so improbable a reading when one considers that it is the Christ-like quality of the lives of saints in general that Cynthia Hahn has argued is the 'controlling force of hagiographic narrative'.[104] She asserts that the 'true subject of the saint's life is not the saint himself but Christ', a point that Gregory of Tours made centuries ago. Here, in this late-twelfth-century frontispiece to the *Life of Cuthbert*, the ambivalence between Christ and Saint is cleverly acknowledged.

But there is another important aspect of the image, namely the way in which Cuthbert is literally depicted. He is a late-twelfth-century bishop, not a prior nor a hermit. He would, in other words, look remarkably similar, at least in his costume, to Hugh du Puiset in a liturgical setting. One should not underestimate this visual resonance. The prostrate monk does not just adore Cuthbert, he venerates Cuthbert-as-bishop, and is, therefore, deferring to the authority of Cuthbert, not simply as saint, or as Christ-type, but as bishop. It is, therefore, possible and credible to suggest that the image was intended to legitimize Puiset's authority as bishop and as the rightful successor to Cuthbert, who, like him, was freely elected by the community of monks.

Finally, there is an additional fact that would seem to point towards the Bishop as patron rather than the monks. There is one scene that has been left out of this manuscript, a scene which was included in the previous illustrated *Life*: the scene of Cuthbert washing the monks' feet illustrating Chapter 18. If the monks, or an individual monk, had commissioned this manuscript, why leave out this touching and revealing scene? Its deletion is more in keeping with the attitude of Puiset, and would only have served to remind him of the special relationship between Cuthbert and the community of monks at Lindisfarne – a relationship that Puiset certainly did not enjoy with the community of monks at Durham at that time.

Conclusion

The production of art and architecture in Durham between 1170 and *c.*1185 can be understood as a response to attempts made by the monastic community and Bishop Hugh du Puiset to revitalize the cult of St Cuthbert. Such a promotion was undertaken for the precise reason that Cuthbert's primacy as a national and regional saint was being undermined and threatened by the rising cult of Becket in the South.

The hagiographical 'evidence' written by Reginald of Durham and the anonymous author of the book of Cuthbert's birth make it clear that a conscious attempt was being made by Reginald and the larger monastic community to reformulate Cuthbert and make his shrine and Durham an appealing place for pilgrims to visit. As Reginald implies, this was being done in direct response to Becket's cult. This literary culture helped to create a more humane and worldly portrait of Cuthbert, and to establish a new hermit saint for Durham in Godric of Finchale.

The revitalization of a cult was an expensive and complex process. It involved a variety of people with a common purpose and the funds to achieve their objectives. In the case of Durham, both the community of monks (including key figures such as Reginald) and Bishop Puiset had a vested interest in maintaining and promoting their patron saint through the troubled decade of the 1170s and into the 1180s. They responded by aggressively promoting Durham and Cuthbert through architectural building campaigns and artistic elaboration of the architectural fabric and the production of manuscripts.

Central to this campaign was the Bishop himself. By constructing the Galilee Chapel, the hospital, and a bridge, and by commissioning the wall paintings of the Galilee and introducing elaborate vestments and beautiful objects to the liturgical proceedings of Durham Cathedral, Puiset was creating an ornate and spectacular environment for pilgrims to experience while visiting the shrine of Cuthbert. In so doing, he also fortified his position in relation to the monastic community. By having Cuthbert represented as a late-twelfth-century Bishop – in other words, as Puiset might have looked during grand liturgical celebrations – Puiset was effectively placing himself in the position as the rightful successor to the patron saint.

Cuthbert survived the crisis of the late-twelfth century, perhaps not as the national saint he was or might have been, but as a saint whose home was now securely located in the North of England, and whose body, incorrupt and softly breathing, lay quietly at the East end of Durham Cathedral. Puiset lived on as well, despite the clandestine activities of the monks. He had helped in the promotion of Cuthbert's cult and managed to do it to his own advantage. His career, by 1175, was in full swing and would last for another twenty years, during which time his opulent habits would become even more pronounced. Godric lived on as well, although he never challenged Cuthbert's primacy to any great degree; he did, however, serve his function. And, of course, Thomas Becket was canonized. Becket had his own story, and although his was played out in Canterbury, he was, in many ways, central to the events in Durham.

Like many saints in the Middle Ages, St Cuthbert was created and recreated in the hagiographical writings of historians and in the imagination of pious pilgrims. In the late twelfth century it was Reginald, the community of monks and Bishop Puiset who refashioned him. Reginald made him almost real and alive, with blood flowing through his veins, even though his coffin had not been opened for seventy years. However, his Cuthbert was a literary one, without corporeal presence or physical identity. It was Hugh du Puiset who gave Cuthbert a body and a face, and it is the wonderful images of Yates Thompson MS 26 which most vividly depict Cuthbert within the mirror of Puiset's aspirations.

In 1827 James Raine found the decomposed body of the saint in the coffin at the East end of Durham Cathedral. With that discovery something of the mystery and spectacle of the shrine vanished. However, Raine did manage to recover objects associated with the body, such as the precious vestments surrounding the corpse and the garnet pectoral cross, objects which by their very proximity to the saint were invested with power and mystery. Cuthbert's body may be gone but his memory is not, nor is the magnificent Cathedral which housed him, the beautiful objects which adorned his body, or the manuscripts made to honour him.

The Plates

The following forty-six plates are the surviving miniatures from BL Yates Thomson MS 26, the *Life* of St Cuthbert by Bede.

The captions include a brief description of the image, Bede's chapter heading and an excerpt from Bede's text. Translations are taken from Bertram Colgrave's translation of Bede's *Life* of St Cuthbert (see Note on p. 6).

The actual miniatures are approximately 14 x 9.5 cm, although each one differs slightly.

PLATE I

58

Preface

Monk kissing the feet of Cuthbert, 1v

The prologue of the blessed priest Bede to the life of St Cuthbert

PLATE 2

Preface

A tonsured, seated scribe, thought to be Bede, 2

PLATE 3

60

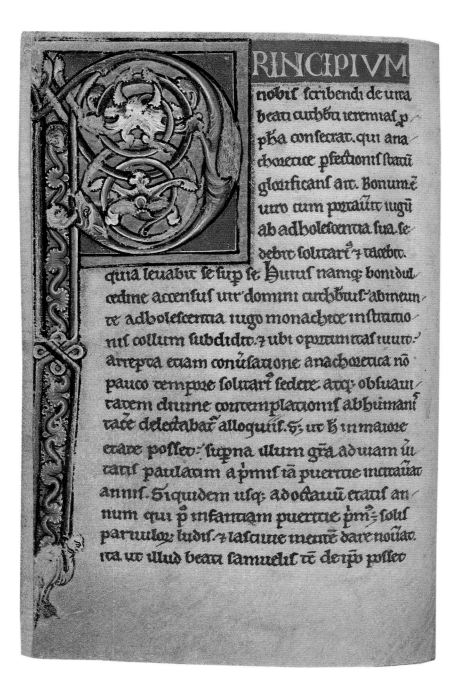

Chapter 2

Initial 'P', 7v

Chapter 3

Cuthbert praying beside the river Tyne, 10v

*How he changed the winds by prayer and brought the rafts,
which had been carried away, safe to land*

*When Cuthbert heard this reply, he knelt down to pray to God, bending his head to the ground,
and immediately the violent wind turned about and bore the rafts safe and sound to land...*

PLATE 5

62

Chapter 3

Two monks praying at the monastery of Tynemouth, 11

Therefore, while the rafts were drifting out to sea, they left the monastery and, gathering on the nearest rock, they knelt down interceding with God on behalf of those whom they perceived to be even now in imminent risk of death.

PLATE 6

Chapter 5

A horse discovers food for the saint, 14

How, while he was on a journey, he received food through God's care

He himself began to spend time in prayer, when suddenly in the midst of his psalm-singing, he saw the horse lift up its head, seize the thatching of the house with its mouth and drag it down. Amid the straw falling from the roof, he saw a folded cloth fall as well – wishing to discover more certainly what it was, he drew near, when his prayer was finished, and found, wrapped in the cloth, half a loaf still warm, and some meat, sufficient for one meal for himself.

PLATE 7

64

Chapter 6

Cuthbert embraced by Boisil at Melrose Abbey, 16

What manner of testimony the holy man Boisil gave to him in the spirit, as he came to the monastery, and how he was received and lived there

And by chance it happened that, having jumped down from his horse on reaching the monastery, and being about to enter the church to pray, he gave both his horse and the spear he was holding to a servant, for he had not yet put off his secular habit...Without saying more, Boisil forthwith kindly received Cuthbert on his arrival, and when the latter had explained the reason of his journey, namely that he preferred the monastery to the world, Boisil still more kindly kept him.

PLATE 8

Chapter 7

Cuthbert washes an angel's feet, 17v

How he entertained an angel and whilst seeking to minister to him earthly bread, was thought worthy to be rewarded by him with heavenly bread

...he found a certain youth sitting within, and, thinking that he was of the race of men, he speedily welcomed him with his accustomed kindness. He gave him water to wash his hands; he washed his feet and wiped them with a towel and placed them in his bosom so as to chaff them humbly with his hands...

PLATE 9

66

Chapter 7

The miraculous loaves from paradise, 18

*As he entered [the storehouse], he immediately encountered a wonderfully fragrant odour.
Looking round to see whence so sweet an odour had arisen, he saw hear by three warm loaves of
unusual whiteness and excellence. And trembling, he said to himself: 'I see that it was an
angel of God who I received and that he came to feed and not to be fed. Behold, he has
brought loaves such as the earth cannot produce; for they excel the lily in whiteness,
the rose in fragrance, and honey in taste. Hence it follows that they have not
come from this earth of ours but they have been brought
from the paradise of joy...'*

PLATE 10

Chapter 8

Cuthbert talking to Boisil, 21

*How Cuthbert was healed of sickness and how Boisil, when he was about to die,
prophesied things which were to come to him*

*Cuthbert, never doubting the truth of his words, answered: 'And what, I ask you, is it best for
me to read, which I can yet finish in one week?' He replied: 'The evangelist John. I have a book
consisting of seven gatherings of which we can get through one every day, with the Lord's help,
reading it and discussing it between ourselves so far as it is necessary.'*

PLATE 11

Chapter 9

Cuthbert preaching, 22v

How Cuthbert was diligent in the ministry of the word

Now it was the custom at that time amongst the English people, when a clerk or a priest came to a village, for all to gather together at his command to hear the word, gladly listening to what was said, and still more gladly following up by their deeds what they could hear and understand...he would tarry in the mountains, summoning the rustics to heavenly things by the words of his preaching as well as by example of his virtue.

PLATE 12

Chapter 10

Cuthbert praying in the sea and his feet wiped by otters, 24

How the animals of the sea, in which he had passed the night in prayer, ministered to him when he came out, and how a brother who saw it, being ill through fear, was restored by his prayers

Cuthbert left the monastery with the spy following him and went down to the sea, above whose shores the monastery was built; going into the deep water until the swelling waves rose as far as his neck and arms, he spent the dark hours of the night watching and singing praises to the sound of the waves. When daybreak was at hand, he went up on to the land and began to pray once more, kneeling on the shore. While he was doing this, there came forth from the depths of the sea two four-footed creatures which are commonly called otters. These, prostrate before him on the sand, began to warm his feet with their breath and sought to dry him with their fur, and when they had finished their ministrations they received his blessing and slipped away into their native waters.

PLATE 13

70

Chapter 11

Cuthbert in a boat, 26

How he promised the sailors who were cut off by the storm that the sea would be calm by a certain day, and how his prayer for food was answered

Now at a certain time, having left the monastery on account of some necessity which arose, he came by boat to the land of the Picts who are called Niduari, accompanied by two brethren, one of whom afterwards became a priest.

PLATE 14

Chapter 11

Cuthbert with a dolphin, 26v

With these words he led them to the shore on which he was accustomed to spend the night in prayer. And when they came there, they found three pieces of dolphin's flesh looking as though some human hand had cut and prepared them for cooking; and kneeling down they gave thanks to God.

PLATE 15

72

Chapter 12

A fish is shared out, 28v

How, while making a journey, he prophesied that he would receive provisions on the way by the ministration of an eagle, and how it came to pass

...suddenly they see an eagle settling on the bank; and the man of God said: 'Do you see where our handmaiden, as I foretold, is settling? Run, I pray you, and see what food she has brought us from the Lord, and bring it quickly here' He ran up and brought a large fish which the eagle had just taken from the river. But the man of God said: 'What have you done, my son? Why have you not given our handmaiden her share? Cut it quickly in half and take her the share which she deserves for ministering to us.'

PLATE 16

Chapter 13

Cuthbert driving away a demon, 30

*How, when he was preaching to the people, he suddenly foresaw that a phantom fire would
come from the devil, and how he extinguished it when it came*

*And with these words he once more took up the thread of the discourse which he had interrupted,
and at once that most evil foe, producing a phantom fire, set light to a house near by, so that
firebrands seemed to be flying all through the village and, fanned by the wind, their crackling rent
the air. Then almost the whole crowd that he was teaching leapt up intending to extinguish the fire,
although he himself kept back a few with outstretched hand: the rest eagerly threw on water,
but with their real water they could not extinguish the false flames, until at the prayers of
Cuthbert the man of God, the author of lies was put to flight, carrying with him his
phantom fires into the empty air.*

PLATE 17

74

Chapter 14

Cuthbert praying at the fire, 31v

How by his prayers he checked the flames of a certain house which was really on fire

Immediately he went out and cast himself upon the ground in front of the door; and while he was still praying, the winds changed and, blowing from the west, removed all danger of the fire attacking the house which the man of God had entered.

PLATE 18

Chapter 15

Cuthbert heals the wife of Hildmaer, 33v

How he drove out a demon from the wife of a reeve, even before his arrival

*And the woman, being loosed from the demon's chains, thereupon rose as if awakened from a deep
sleep and, running to greet the man of God, she took the horse on which he was seated by the bridle:
and having wholly recovered her strength both of mind and body, she prayed him to dismount
quickly and to enter and bless her home; and offering him devoted service, she openly
testified how, as soon as she touched his bridle, she felt herself to be freed from all
the trouble of her old affliction.*

PLATE 19

76

Chapter 16

Cuthbert teaching the monks at Lindisfarne, 35v

How he lived and taught in the monastery in Lindisfarne

*Now there were certain brethren in the monastery who preferred to conform to their older usage
rather than to the monastic rule. Nevertheless he overcame these by his modest virtue and patience,
and by daily effort he gradually converted them to a better state of mind. In fact, very often
during debates in the chapter of the brethren concerning the rule, when he was assailed by
the bitter insults of his opponents, he would rise up suddenly and with calm mind
and countenance would go out...*

PLATE 20

Chapter 17

Cuthbert making his hermitage with the help of an angel, 39

How he drove out the demons and made himself a dwelling in the island of Farne

Some of these stones were so great that it would seem to have been scarcely possible for four men to have lifted them, but nevertheless he was found to have brought them thither from elsewhere with angelic aid, and to have placed them in the wall.

PLATE 21

Chapter 18

___

Cuthbert digging with a monk, 41

How he produced water from dry land by his prayers and how he lived as a hermit

*So they made a pit and on the next day they found it full of water which came from within.
Hence there was no doubt that this water had been drawn from ground which before had been
exceedingly dry and hard, through the prayers of the man of God.*

PLATE 22

Chapter 19

Cuthbert expelling birds, 42v

*How, with a word, he drove away the birds from the crops which he had
sown with his own hand*

*And when it had begun to ripen, some birds came and eagerly set about consuming it... 'Why', said
he, 'do you touch the crops that you did not sow? Or is it, perchance, that you have greater need of
them than I? If, however, you have received permission from God, do what He has allowed you;
but if not, depart and do not injure any more the possessions of another.'*

PLATE 23

Chapter 20

Crows pick thatch and bring lard to Cuthbert, 44

*How the ravens atoned for the injury which they had done to the man of God
by their prayers and by a gift*

*...one day, as they were building their nests, the man of God saw them tear with their beaks the
little guest-house of the brethren ... and carry off in their bills the straw with which it was
thatched, as material for their nests.....Now when three days had passed, one of the pair returned
and found the servant of Christ digging. With its feathers sadly ruffled and its head drooping to its
feet, and with humble cries it prayed for pardon, using such signs as it could...Without delay they*
[it and its mate] *both returned bringing a worthy gift, namely a portion of hog's lard.*

PLATE 24

Chapter 21

Cuthbert discovers the roof beam, 45v

How even the sea ministered to his necessities

*They did as he said and rising up in the morning, they saw that the night tide had carried up
some timber of the required length, and placed it over the very spot whereon it was to be set for the
building. As soon as they saw this, they marveled at the holiness of the venerable man
for whom even the elements did service...*

PLATE 25

82

Chapter 22

Cuthbert with a crowd, 47

*How he gave instruction in the way of salvation to many who came to him and showed
the weakness of the snares of the ancient foe*

*Now many came to the man of God, not only from the neighbourhood of Lindisfarne but also from
the remoter parts of Britain...*[Cuthbert said] *'Boisil... predicted with prophetic truth all
the things which were to happen to me. And of all those things which he predicted to me,
only one remains, which I would might never be fulfilled.'*
[That he be elected to the office of bishop]

PLATE 26

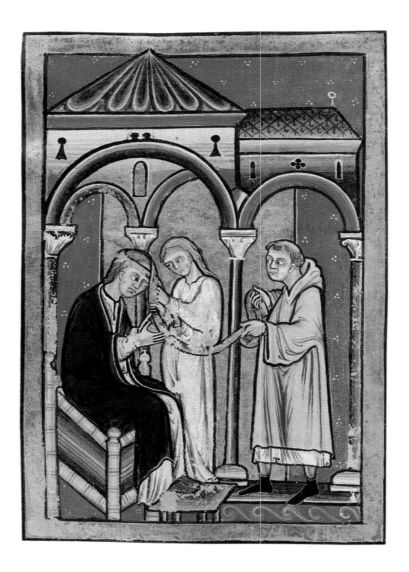

Chapter 23

Aelfflaed cured by Cuthbert's girdle, 48v

How the abbess Aelfflaed and one of her nuns were healed by means of his girdle

Seeing her grievously afflicted, she brought this same girdle of the man of God and had it bound around her head: on that same day the pain departed and she was healed. The abbess, however, took away the girdle and placed it in her box [from whence it disappeared].

PLATE 27

Chapter 24

Aelfflaed meets Cuthbert, 50v

*How, in answer to the same Aelfflaed, he made predictions about the life of King Ecgfrith
and about his own bishopric*

*Having got into conversation with him, and having heard much from him on the matters about
which she was asking him, suddenly, in the midst of their talk, she fell at his feet and adjured him
by the terrible awe-inspiring name of the King of Heaven and of his angels, that he would tell her
how long Ecgfrith her brother would live and rule over the kingdom of the English.*

PLATE 28

Chapter 24

Ecgfrith visits Cuthbert, 51

And when he could by no means be dragged from his place by the many messengers and letters that were sent to him, at length this same king himself, together with the most holy bishop Trumwine, as well as many other religious and powerful men, sailed to the island.

PLATE 29

86

Chapter 24

Cuthbert at synod, 53v

When he had come [to the synod], *in spite of his reluctance he was overcome by the unanimous will of them all and compelled to submit his neck to the yoke of the bishopric.*

PLATE 30

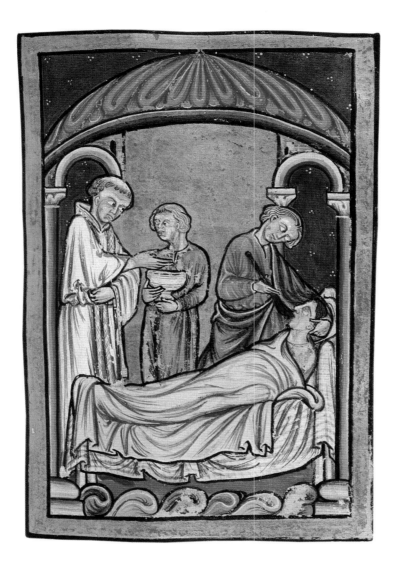

Chapter 25

Cuthbert blessing water and a cure, 54

*How, when he was elected to the bishopric, he cured the ailing servant of a gesith
with holy water*

*He immediately blessed some water and gave it to the servant of the gesith...the man of God gave
him the holy water saying: 'Go and give it to the sick man to take.' He obeyed his words and
brought the water to the sick man...when his master visited him in the morning, he was
found to be cured.*

PLATE 31

88

Chapter 27

Cuthbert and Ecgfrith's widow, 55v

*How, though absent, he saw in spirit the destruction of King Ecgfrith and of his army,
in accordance with his own prediction*

*On the next day, while the citizens were conducting him to see the walls of the city and a
marvelously constructed fountain of Roman workmanship, he was suddenly troubled in spirit,
and as he stood leaning on his staff he turned his face sadly towards the ground; and again,
standing upright and lifting his eyes towards heaven, he sighed deeply and said in a low voice:
'Perhaps even now the issue of the battle is decided.'*

PLATE 32

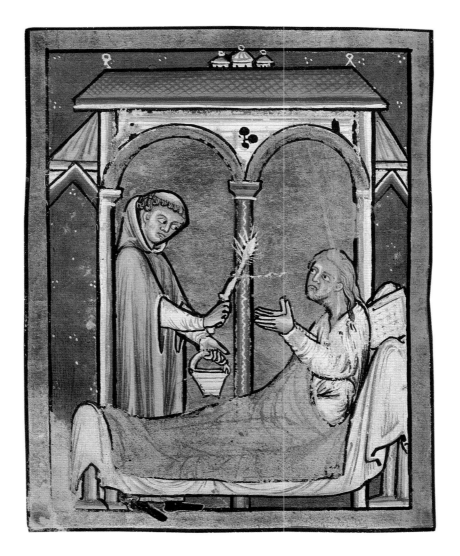

Chapter 29

Healing a gesith's wife, 58v

How through his priest he cured the wife of a gesith with holy water

He entered the sleeping chamber in which she lay like one dead, sprinkled her and her bed and, opening her mouth, poured in a portion of health-giving draught. A wonderful and exceedingly amazing thing happened – as soon as the blessed water touched the sick woman, though it was done without her knowledge, she yet received full healing of mind and body…

PLATE 33

Chapter 30

Healing a girl, 60

How he cured a girl of pains in the head and the side by anointing her with oil

...for all through the year she had been troubled with an intolerable pain in the head and in the whole of one side, and had entirely been given up by the physicians. When those who had come with him told the man of God about her and prayed for her restoration, he had pity on her and anointed the wretched woman with holy oil. She began to get better that very hour and after a few days was restored to complete health.

PLATE 34

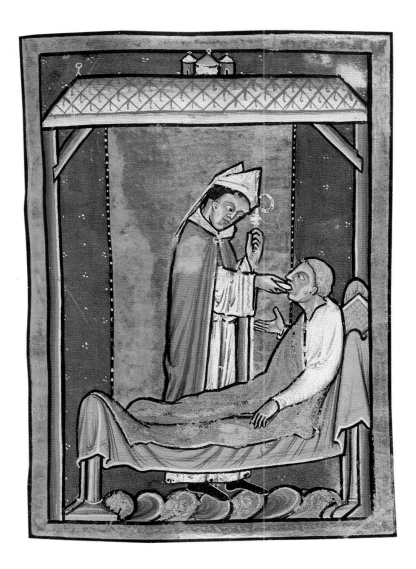

Chapter 31

Healing a man, 61

How a sick man was healed with bread which he had blessed

*Nor do we consider that we ought to pass over in silence a miracle, as we have learned,
was performed by the virtue of the same venerable man, though he himself was absent...suddenly
one of them recalled that he had some bread with him, which Cuthbert, the man of the Lord, had
recently blessed and given to him...they filled a cup with water and put in a very little of the bread,
and gave to him to drink. No sooner had the draught of water, sanctified by the bread,
reached his stomach, than all the inward pain had disappeared...*

PLATE 35

92

Chapter 33

Healing a child, 62v

How, during the time of the plague, he restored a dying boy in sound health to his mother

The priest pointed her out to the man of God, who did not delay but, approaching her and giving
her his blessing, kissed the boy and said to his mother: 'Do not fear nor be sad;
for your infant will be healed and live, nor will anyone else be missing
from your home through this plague.'

PLATE 36

Chapter 34

Fall from a tree, 63v

How he beheld the soul of a certain man, who was killed by falling from a tree,
being carried to heaven

PLATE 37

94

Chapter 34

Cuthbert's vision, 64

*The limbs of his body relaxed and lost their function, the colour of his face changed, and his eyes
were fixed against their wont as if in amazement, while the knife he was holding fell to the
table...But when she adjured him and importuned him more earnestly to reveal his vision, he said:
'I have seen the soul of a certain holy man being carried by the hands of angels to the joys of the
heavenly kingdom'...On asking who it was, he learned that one of the shepherds,
a man of good life, climbing a tree too incautiously had fallen down, and his body
was so injured that he breathed forth his spirit at the very hour in which the
man of God had seen it carried to heaven.*

PLATE 38

Chapter 35

Cuthbert passing wine, 66

How, by tasting water, he gave it the flavour of wine

After they had risen from their midday rest, he asked for something to drink, saying that he was thirsty. 'Give me water,' he said. So they brought him water drawn from the well. Having blessed it and drunk a little of it, he gave it to his priest who was standing by, who gave it to a servant.

PLATE 39

Chapter 38

Cuthbert takes a monk on to his boat, 71v

How though sick himself he healed his attendant of diarrhoea

And when his illness increased and he saw that the time of his departure was at hand,
he commanded that he should be carried back to his little dwelling-place and oratory...
So we carried him thither because, owing to the pain of his disease, he could not walk...
And looking round us all, he saw the brother whom I mentioned before, who suffered
from diarrhoea, and he said: 'Let Walhstod...enter with me...'

PLATE 40

Chapter 39

The death of Cuthbert, 73

Of his last commands to his brethren and how, when he had received the viaticum,
he yielded up his spirit in prayer

But when the accustomed time of nightly prayer arrived, he received from me the sacraments
of salvation and fortified himself for his death, which he knew had now come, by the
communion of the Lord's body and blood; and, raising his eyes to heaven and stretching
out his hands aloft, he sent forth his spirit in the very act of praising God to the
joys of the heavenly Kingdom.

PLATE 41

Chapter 40

Signaling the death by torches, 74v

How, in accordance with the prophecy of the psalm which they had been singing when he died, the Lindisfarne brethren were attacked, but, with the help of the Lord, were protected

'I immediately went out and announced his death to the brethren who had passed the night in watching and prayers...Without delay one of them ran out and lit two torches: and holding one in each hand, he went on to some higher ground to show the brethren who were in the Lindisfarne monastery that his holy soul had gone to be with the Lord.'

PLATE 42

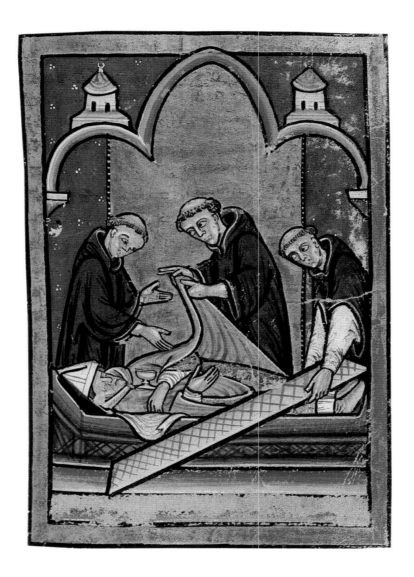

Chapter 42

Discovery of the incorrupt body, 77

How his body was found incorrupt eleven years afterwards

*...and opening the sepulchre, they found the body intact and whole, as if it were still alive,
and the joints of the limbs flexible, and much more like a sleeping than a dead man.
Moreover all his garments, in which he had been clothed, were not only undefiled but
seemed to be perfectly new and wondrously bright.*

PLATE 43

Chapter 44

Sick man healed at the tomb, 79

How a sick man was cured by praying at his tomb

*He did as he had asked and with no small effort led the sick man, leaning on his staff, into the
church. He bent his knees at the sepulchre of the most holy father, beloved of God,
and with head bowed to the ground he prayed for recovery.*

PLATE 44

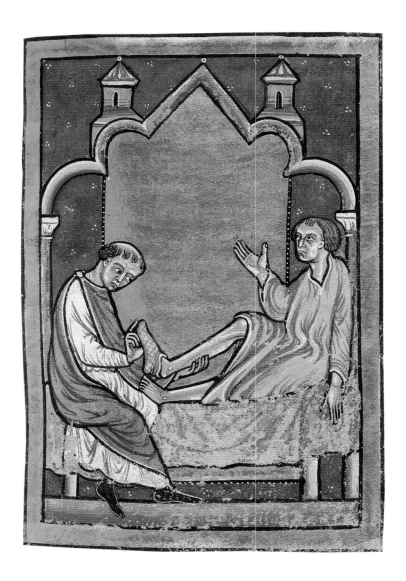

Chapter 45

Man healed by shoes, 80

How a paralytic was healed by his shoes

He therefore asked his servant to bring some portion of the incorruptible relics of the sacred body because he believed that, by the bounty of the Lord, he might return to the grace of health through its virtues. And having consulted the abbot, the servant brought the shoes which had been upon the feet of the man of God in the sepulchre and put them upon the nerveless feet of the sick man – for the paralysis had first seized him in his feet.

PLATE 45

102

45

Historia ecclesiastica, bk. iv, 31–32

Cuthbert's arm emerges from the tomb to cure paralytic, 83

While he was praying he seemed to fall into a deep sleep and, as he afterwards used to relate, he felt a great broad hand touch his head where the pain lay; the touch also passed over all that part of the body which had been afflicted by the disease, right down to his feet.

PLATE 46

46

Historia ecclesiastica, bk. iv, 32

Youth's eye healed, 84v

[A brother] *received the hairs of the holy head and, moved by a timely impulse, applied them to his diseased eyelid, trying for some time to reduce and soften the swelling by their application... he suddenly touched his eye about midday and found that the eyelid was as sound as if there had never been any deformity or tumour on it.*

Abbreviations

A-ND	*Anglo-Norman Durham 1093–1193*, David Rollason, Margaret Harvey and Michael Prestwich eds (Woodbridge, 1994)
Cat.Vet.	*Catalogi Veteres Librorum Ecclesiae Dunelmensis*, J. Raine ed. (SS, 1838)
Cuthbert	*St Cuthbert, His Cult and His Community to A.D. 1200*, Gerald Bonner, David Rollason, and Claire Stancliffe eds (Woodbridge, 1989)
DCL	Durham, Dean and Chapter Library
DCM	R.A.B. Mynors, *Durham Cathedral Manuscripts to the end of the Twelfth Century* (Oxford, 1939).
FPD	*Feodarium Prioratus Dunelmensis*, W. Greenwell ed. (SS 58, 1871)
Libellus	Reginald of Durham's *'Little Book' about the Wonderful Miracles of Blessed Cuthbert which were performed in Recent Times*, cited by chapter; J. Raine ed., *Reginaldi monachi Dunelmensis Libellus de admirandis beati Cuthberti virtutibus quae novellis patratae sunt*

	temporibus (SS 1, 1835). Page references, where necessary are to this edition
PL	*Patrologiae cursus completus, series latina*, J.P. Migne ed. (221 vols.; Paris, 1844–64)
Relics	C.F. Battiscombe ed., *The Relics of St Cuthbert* (Oxford, 1956)
RS	Roll Series (Rerum Britannicarum medii Aevi Scriptores or Chronicles and Memorials of Great Britain and Ireland during the Middle Ages)
Scammell	G.V. Scammell, *Hugh du Puiset Bishop of Durham* (Cambridge, 1956)
Scriptores Tres	*Historia Dunelmensis Scriptores Tres*, J. Raine ed. (SS 9, 1839)
SS	Surtees Society
Two Lives	Bertram Colgrave, *Two Lives of Saint Cuthbert* (Cambridge, 1940)
V.Godr.	*Libellus de vita et miraculis S. Godrici, hermitae de Finachle, auctore Reginaldo monacho Dunelmensi*, Joseph Stevenson ed. (SS 20, 1847)

Appendix

Description of Yates Thompson MS 26

British Library, Yates Thompson MS 26. THE LIFE OF ST CUTHBERT. The prose *Life* of St Cuthbert written by Bede with additional texts from Symeon of Durham. Written and illuminated in Durham; late twelfth century (*c.*1180/5), on palaeographical and art historical grounds. Edited and translated by Bertram Colgrave, *Two Lives of Saint Cuthbert* (Cambridge, 1940).

Parchment; fols vi + 150. *Secundo folio* 'dubiorum'. 134 mm x 97 mm. Pricked and ruled in lead point for one column of 23 lines (above top line) with double bounding lines. Gatherings (15) as follows: 1^{12} (1 cancelled); 2^{12} wants 3; $3–5^{12}$ wants 9; 6^{12} wants 1, 6, 12; 7^{12} wants 2, 11; 8^{12} wants 4, 7; 9^{6}; 10^{12}; 11^{10}; 12^{12}; 13^{6}; 14^{12}; 15^{6}. Modern Arabic numerals used for the foliation. Several faint quire signatures in a larger, possibly seventeenth century, hand in the lower centre margin. There are no indications or remnants of catchwords nor of roman numerals in the margins to denote the quire signatures as was the custom in the Durham scriptorium at this date. However, it may be that once the manuscript was cropped it lost the numerals. Evidence that the manuscript was cropped can be found on folio 127 where a secondary initial has been cropped. Consecutive letters of the alphabet (c, g, h, k, x, y, and z) written in a small neat hand, possibly contemporary with the main text, remain in the lower centre margin between folios 38 and 52.

Contents:
1. fol. 2v. Letter to Bishop Eadfrith from Bede.
2. fol. 4r. Letter to the priest John from Bede.
3. fol. 5r. Capitula.
4. fol. 7v. Bede's prose *Life of Saint Cuthbert*.
5. fol. 83v. Excerpts from Bede's *Historia Ecclesiastica*, lib. iv, capp. 29, 30.
6. fol. 87r. History of the Translation of St Cuthbert by Symeon of Durham.
7. fol. 130r. Extracts from the *Historia Dunelmensis Ecclesiae* by Symeon of Durham.
8. fol. 146r. The Relatio de S. Cuthberto.
9. fol. 149r. An account of the early Provosts of Hexham.

The decoration consists of the following:
1. Monk kissing the feet of Cuthbert, 1v
2. A tonsured, seated scribe, thought to be Bede 2
3. Initial 'D', 2v
4. Initial 'P', 7v
5. Cuthbert praying beside the river Tyne 10v
6. Two monks praying at the monastery of Tynemouth, 11
7. A horse discovers food for the saint, 14
8. Cuthbert embraced by Boisil at Melrose Abbey, 16
9. Cuthbert washes an angel's feet, 17v
10. The miraculous loaves from paradise, 18
11. Cuthbert talking to Boisil, 21
12. Cuthbert preaching, 22v
13. Cuthbert praying in the sea and his feet wiped by otters, 24
14. Cuthbert in a boat, 26
15. Cuthbert with dolphin, 26v
16. A fish is shared out, 28v
17. Cuthbert drives away a demon, 30
18. Cuthbert praying at the fire, 31v
19. Cuthbert heals the wife of Hildmaer, 33v
20. Cuthbert teaching the monks at Lindisfarne, 35v
21. Cuthbert making his hermitage with the help of an angel, 39
22. Cuthbert digging with a monk, 41
23. Cuthbert expelling birds, 42v
24. Crows pick thatch and bring lard to Cuthbert, 44
25. Cuthbert discovers the roof beam, 45v
26. Cuthbert with a crowd, 47
27. Aelfflaed cured by Cuthbert's girdle, 48v
28. Aelfflaed meets Cuthbert, 50v
29. Ecgfrith visits Cuthbert, 51
30. Cuthbert at synod, 53v
31. Cuthbert blessing water and a cure, 54
32. Cuthbert and Ecgfrith's widow, 55v
33. Healing a gesith's wife, 58v
34. Healing a girl, 60
35. Healing a man, 61
36. Healing a child, 62v
37. Fall from a tree, 63v
38. Cuthbert's vision, 64
39. Cuthbert passing wine, 66
40. Cuthbert takes a monk on to his boat, 71v
41. The death of Cuthbert, 73
42. Signaling the death by torches, 74v
43. Discovery of the incorrupt body, 77
44. Sick man healed at the tomb, 79
45. Man healed by shoes, 80
46. Cuthbert's arm emerges from the tomb to cure paralytic, 83
47. Youth's eye healed, 84v

Notes

1   *Two Lives*.

2   *Two Lives*; *Vita S. Cuthberti Metrica*, W. Jaager ed., *Palaestra*, 198, 1935; *Historia Ecclesiastica* IV.27–32, 274–80.

3   *Two Lives*, pp. 3–10, 13, and B. Colgrave, 'St Cuthbert and his Times', in *Relics*, pp. 115–43.

4   Gregory of Tours explained this relationship when he said: 'some ask whether we should say the life of the saints or the lives of the saints.' He maintained that the singular is the best form, that is the life of the saints, 'because thought there may be some difference in their merits and virtues, yet the life of one body [Christ's] nourished them all in this world.' Quoted in Cynthia Hahn, 'Picturing the Text: Narrative in the *Life* of the Saints', *Art History*, Vol. 13, No. 1, 1990, p. 6 and note 28.

5   Alan Thacker, 'Bede's Ideal of Reform', *Ideal and Reality in Frankish and Anglo-Saxon Society*, P. Wormald ed. (Oxford, 1983), p. 137.

6   The earlier metrical *Life*, written between 705 and 716, was quite similar to the anonymous *Life*, and therefore offers little contrast. See Michael Lapidge, 'Bede's Metrical *Vita S. Cuthberti*' in *Cuthbert*, pp. 77–94 and Alan Thacker, 'Lindisfarne and the Origins of the Cult of St Cuthbert' in *Cuthbert*, pp. 103–124.

7   In chapter 6, Bede explains how conscientious Cuthbert was in his duties as monk. In chapter 9, Bede recalls how, upon the death of Boisil, Cuthbert took the office of prior, and in chapter 22 Boisil's deathbed prophecy was fulfilled as Cuthbert, trembling at the thought of taking it, agreed to accept the bishopric. *Two Lives*, Chapters 6, 9, 16, 22, 26, pp. 172–74, 184–86, 206–12, 228–30, 240–42.

8   Thacker, 'Bede's Ideal of Reform', p. 142. *Two Lives*, Chp. 26, pp. 240–42.

9   Walter Berschin, '*Opus deliberatum ac perfectum*: Why Did the Venerable Bede Write a Second Prose Life of Cuthbert?' in *A-ND*, pp. 95–103.

10 Corpus christianorum, series latina (Turnhout, 1953 –) 122, p.189. See Berschin, '*Opus*', page 101, note 15.

11 Anna Muthesius, 'Silks and Saints: The Rider and Peacock Silks from the Relics of St Cuthbert' in *Cuthbert*, pp. 343–365.

12 Elizabeth Coatsworth, 'The Pectoral Cross and Portable altar from the Tomb of St Cuthbert' in *Cuthbert*, pp. 287–302.

13 Michelle P. Brown, 'The Lindisfarne Scriptorium from the Late Seventh to the Early Ninth Century' in *Cuthbert*, pp. 151–164. Janet Backhouse, *The Lindisfarne Gospels* (Oxford, 1981) with bibliography.

14 The process of 'sacralizing space' in this manner is not new. In 1989 the remains of King Lazar, a medieval Serbian leader, were taken from monastery to monastery in the Serbian territory to mark the borders of the symbolic Serbian community. See David Campbell, 'Violence, Justice, and Identity in the Bosnian Conflict' in *Sovereignty and Subjectivity*, Jenny Edkins, Nalini Persram and Véronique Pin-Fat eds (Boulder; London, 1999), pp. 21–37.

15 D.W. Rollason, 'Why was St Cuthbert so Popular?', *Cuthbert Saint and Patron* (Durham, 1987), pp. 9–22. For a discussion on the historical background see B. Colgrave, 'St Cuthbert', pp. 115–143.

16 Thacker, 'Bede's Idea of Reform', pp. 136–42 and 148–50 and Thacker, 'Lindisfarne and the Origins', pp. 103–122.

17 Helen M. Jewell, *The North-South Divide. The Origins of Northern Consciousness in England* (Manchester; New York, 1994), p. 28. See also Rosemary Cramp, 'The Northumbrian Identity' in *Northumbria's Golden Age*, Jane Hawkes and Susan Mills eds, (Gloucestershire, 1999), pp. 1–11.

18 Eddius Stephanus, 'Life of Wilfrid', J.F. Webb trans., in *The Age of Bede*, D.H. Farmer ed. (Harmondsworth, 1983), p. 182.

19 Eddius Stephanus, 'Life of Wilfrid', p. 127.

20 S. Keynes and M. Lapidge eds, *Alfred the Great* (Harmondsworth, 1983), p. 125.

21 *Alfred the Great*, p. 125.

22 Henry of Huntingdon, *Chronicle*, T. Forester ed. (London, 1853), p. 152.

23 Henry of Huntingdon, *Chronicle*, p. 173.

24 William of Malmesbury, 'History of the Kings', *Church Historians*, III, 1, pp. 39, 59, 60–61, 124, 253.

25 William of Malmesbury, 'History', pp. 198–9.

26 M. Chibnall, *Anglo-Norman England 1066–1166* (Oxford, 1990), pp. 16, 49, 50.

27 See William M. Aird, *St Cuthbert and the Normans. The Church of Durham, 1071–1153*, (Woodbridge, 1998); Scammell, pp. 183–241; and H.E. Craster, 'The patrimony of St Cuthbert', *English Historical Review*, 69, 1954.

28 William M. Aird, *St Cuthbert*, p. 5.

29   S.J. Ridyard, '*Condigna Veneratio*: Post-Conquest Attitudes to the Saints of the Anglo-Saxons' in *Anglo-Norman Studies* IX, p. 196.

30   Thomas Arnold ed., *Symeonis Monachi Opera Omnia*, 2 Vols., Roll Series 1882–85, pp. 99–100.

31   *Symeonis Monachi Opera Omnia*, p.106.

32   *Symeonis Monachi Opera Omnia*, p.107.

33   Malcolm Thurlby, 'The Building of the Cathedral: the Romanesque and Early Gothic Fabric', in *Durham Cathedral. A Celebration*, Douglas Pocock ed. (Durham, 1993), p. 15.

34   *Symeonis Monachi Opera Omnia*, vol. I, 1882, pp. 247–61; vol. II, 1885, pp. 359–62. For Reginald's account see *Libellus*, especially pp. 111–12. See also Bertram Colgrave, 'The Post-Bedan Miracles and Translations of Saint Cuthbert', *The Early Cultures of North-West Europe* (H.M. Chadwick Memorial Studies), Cambridge, 1950, pp. 329–31.

35   T.J. Brown ed., *The Stonyhurst Gospel of St John* (Oxford, 1969) and, recently, Michelle P. Brown, 'The Lindisfarne Scriptorium', p. 151–165, especially p. 153.

36   *PL* 35, 1443. For a discussion of the use of St John's Gospel as talisman see Brown, *The Stonyhurst Gospel*, 30ff. See also Edmond Le Blant, 'Le premier chapitre de Saint Jean et la croyance à ses vertus secrètes', *Revue archéologique*, 3rd series xxv, 1894, pp. 8–13.

37   *Libellus*, pp. 111–12.

38   Barabara Abou-el-Haj, *The Medieval Cult of Saints. Formations and Transformations* (Cambridge, 1997) p. 15.

39   Quoted in Abou-el-Haj, p. 17, note 63.

40   For a discussion of the implications of Becket's murder for the cult of Cuthbert in Durham see Dominic Marner, *The Bible of Hugh du Puiset: Authority, Appropriation and Invention in the Late Twelfth Century*, Ph.D. thesis (University of East Anglia, 1995).

41   The primary source of his life is Scammell.

42   For a discussion of Puiset's manuscripts see Marner, *The Bible*.

43   Scammell, p. 10.

44   Roger of Hovedon, *Chronica Magistri Rogeri de Hovedene*, William Stubbs ed. (RS 51, 1868–1871) vol. iii, p. xxxiii.

45   Scammell, p. 133.

46   See David Bates, 'The Forged Charters of William the Conqueror and Bishop William of St Calais', in *A-ND*, pp. 111–124.

47   *Scriptores Tres*, p. 11. Trans. by Richard Halsey, 'The Galilee Chapel' in *Medieval Art and Architecture at Durham Cathedral*, Nicola Coldstream and Peter Draper eds, (Leeds, 1980) pp. 59–73. For the Galilee chapel see also S.A. Harrison, 'Observations on the Architecture of the Galilee Chapel' in *A-ND*, pp. 213–234. W.H.D. Longstaffe, 'Bishop Pudsey's Buildings in the present County of Durham', *Transactions of the Architectural and Archaeological Society of Durham and Northumberland*, ii, 1870, pp. 1ff.; W. White, 'The Galilee', *Royal Institute of British Architects*, Transactions, New. Ser., vi, 1890, pp. 153–64.

48   The first mention of it as the 'Galilee' comes from a charter which dates from 1174–89, and this charter also describes an altar in the Galilee dedicated to the Virgin. See Halsey, 'The Galilee Chapel', p. 61.

49   W. Farrer ed., *Early Yorkshire Charters*, for the Yorkshire Archaeological Society, vol. II, 1915, pp. 286–87.

50   Halsey, 'The Galilee Chapel', p. 61. For a general discussion of the shrine of St Cuthbert see John Crook, 'The Architectural Setting of the Cult of St Cuthbert in Durham Cathedral (1093–1200)' in *A-ND*, pp. 235–250.

51   See S.A. Harrison, 'Observations', pp. 213–34 and E.C. Fernie, 'The Architectural Influence of Durham Cathedral' in *AN-D*, pp. 269–282.

52   There has been some disagreement over the identity of the painted King and Bishop. In 1833 James Raine described them as 'a king and a Bishop, probably Richard I and Pudsey himself'. His attribution was echoed by R.W. Billings in the mid-nineteenth century, George Ornsby in 1846, C.E. Keyser in 1877, and again in 1883. The attribution of the two figures of king and bishop as Oswald and Cuthbert was suggested by Canon Greenwell in 1879. This tentative attribution was accepted as fact by Audrey Baker in 1956 in her article on the frontispiece to *The Relics of St Cuthbert*. Audrey Baker, 'The Frontispiece', in *Relics*, pp. 528–530. M. Johnson has questioned the identification of these figures. See 'The North-East Altar in the Galilee of Durham Cathedral', *Transactions of the Architectural and Archaeological Society of Durham and Northumberland*, xi, 1965, pp. 371–90. M. Johnson and M. McIntyre, 'Wall Paintings in the Galilee of Durham Cathedral', *Transactions of the Architectural and Archaeological Society of Durham and Northumberland*, xi, 1962, pp. 278–80. See also D.H. Farmer, 'Cuthbert' in *Lexikon der christlichen Ikonographie*, E. Kirschbaum and W. Braunfels eds (Freiburg im Breigau, 1974), cols. 8–10. David Park recently stated that the identification of the figures as Oswald and Cuthbert quite simply 'must be correct'. David Park, 'The Interior Decoration of the Cathedral' in *Durham Cathedral. A Celebration*, (Durham, 1993), p. 57. More cautious identifications were given by others including Tristram in his survey of English wall-painting, while Margot Johnson argued that the identification of the figures as Puiset and Richard I or as Cuthbert and Oswald appears to have no foundation and is based on nothing but 'guesswork'. See E.W. Tristram, *English Medieval Wall Painting. The Twelfth Century* (Oxford, 1944), p. 142, supp. pls. 13 a and b. and Johnson, 'The North-East Altar', pp. 371–90.

53   The other is the vision of a man falling from a tree (chapter 34 of the *Life*).

54   Based on the use of the past tense in referring to the events of 1173–74, when William the Lion of Scotland came to the aid of the eldest son of Henry II, Tudor

argued that the finished *Libellus* was completed no earlier than 13 July 1174 (when King William was captured by the English). Victoria Tudor, 'The Cult of St Cuthbert in the Twelfth Century: The Evidence of Reginald of Durham' in *Cuthbert* , p. 449.

55 *Libellus*, chp. 16, 29; chp. 26, 57.

56 Victoria Tudor, 'The Cult of St Cuthbert', p. 453, note 41.

57 Symeon writes, 'When eleven years had passed since the period of his death, the brethren opened his tomb, and found his corpse quite as fresh as if he had been recently buried. The limbs were flexible, and his whole appearance was more like that of a man who was asleep than one dead...', *Scriptores Tres*, Chp. XI.

58 There are, of course, a variety of ways to explain the notion that Cuthbert's body was incorrupt, including the idea that it was an elaborate hoax concocted by an individual or group of people with a vested interest in elevating Cuthbert's saintly status. However, recently, Paul Barber has suggested that the body of Cuthbert was preserved by saponification, which is a form of post mortem change 'in which there is alteration of the appearance and consistency of the fatty tissues of the body consequent upon the transformation of the neutral fat into new compounds, mostly fatty acids'. See Paul Barber, *Vampires, Burial and Death. Folklore and Reality* (New Haven and London, 1988), p. 108

59 Victoria Tudor, 'The Cult of St Cuthbert', especially pp. 449ff.

60 V. Tudor, 'The Misogyny of Saint Cuthbert', *Archaeologia Aeliana*, 5th series, 12, 1984, pp. 157–67.

61 It is certain that they were not permitted in the chapel on the Inner Farne, even though they were allowed in the churchyard. However, in no other church dedicated to Cuthbert was this attitude prevalent. Therefore, it was likely that these misogynistic tendencies were confined to Durham and its monastic community, as well as to the other two closely-related churches — the Inner Farne and the Lindisfarne — which shared in the historic development of the cult of Cuthbert. Victoria Tudor, 'The Cult of St Cuthbert', p. 457.

62 *Libellus*, Chp. 121, pp. 267–8; Chp. 123; Chp. 124.

63 *Scriptores Tres*, 7, p. 11.

64 For a discussion of Cuthbert's 'tougher' side see Victoria Tudor, 'Durham Priory and its Hermits in the Twelfth Century' in *A-ND*, pp. 453ff.

65 *Libellus*, Chp. 62, pp. 248–254.

66 Victoria Tudor, 'Durham Priory', pp. 67–78.

67 Donald Matthew, 'Durham and the Anglo-Norman World' in *A-ND*, p. 17.

68 *V.Godr.*, Chp. 170, p. 331.

69 *V.Godr.* Appendix I, Chp. 22, p. 367.

70 *V.Godr.* Appendix II, Chp. 1, pp. 372–3.

71 *V.Godr.* Appendix II, Chp. 1, p. 372.

72 'Libellus de nativitate sancti Cuthberti de his historiis Hybernensium excerptus et translatus' in *Micellanea Biographica*, James Raine ed. (SS 8; 1838), pp. 61–87. M.H. Dodds, 'The Little Book of the Birth of St Cuthbert', *Archaeologia Aeliana*, 4th series, 6 (1929), pp. 52–94. Also P. Grosjean, 'The Alleged Irish Origin of Saint Cuthbert' in *Relics*, pp. 144–54.

73 The text has a relatively short preface and only twenty-nine chapters. Despite its importance, the preface has received no previous consideration precisely because those concerned are either trying to prove or disprove the Irish origin of Cuthbert, and are less interested in why such a text would have been written in the North in the late twelfth century.

74 For a discussion of the identification of these figures see M.H. Dodds, 'The Little Book', pp. 66–67.

75 H.Y. Thompson, *A Descriptive Catalogue of Twenty Illuminated Manuscripts, Nos. LXXV to LCIV* (Cambridge, 1907), pp. 78–90, no. LXXXIV; British Museum, *Catalogue of Additions to the Manuscripts 1916–20* (London, 1933), pp. 262–5; R.A.B. Mynors, *Durham Cathedral Manuscripts to the end of the Twelfth Century* (Oxford, 1939), p. 77, no. 132; W. Forbes-Leith, *The Life of St Cuthbert* (Edinburgh, 1888); Malcolm Baker, 'Medieval Illustrations of Bede's *Life of St. Cuthbert*', *Journal of the Warburg and Courtauld Institutes* , Vol. 41, 1978, pp. 16–49; N. Morgan, *Early Gothic Manuscripts I, 1190–1250. A Survey of Manuscripts Illuminated in the British Isles*, Vol. 4, (London, 1982), pp. 57–9, ills. 38–43.

76 The London manuscript corresponds to the Durham medieval library catalogue entry: 'Vita Sancti Cuthberti et miracula eiusdem curiosa illuminata, ii fo dubiorum', *Cat.Vet.*, p. 29.

77 *Two Lives*, p. 50.

78 Michelle P. Brown, *A Guide to Western Historical Scripts from Antiquity to 1600* (London and Toronto, 1990).

79 T.S.R. Boase, *English Art 1100–1216* (Oxford, 1953), pp. 287–8, pls 93b and d.

80 Baker, 'Medieval Illustrations', pp. 21–22.

81 O. Pächt and J.J.G. Alexander, *Illuminated Manuscripts in the Bodleian Library, Oxford*, iii (Oxford, 1973), p. 224, no. 221, pl. xxii.

82 For a discussion of the application of paneled frames see Dominic Marner, *The Bible*, Chapter Two.

83 A change in scribal hand occurs on 129v/130.

84 Malcolm Baker published a superb article on the medieval pictorial cycles of the *Life of St Cuthbert* in 1978. The following analysis of the images in Yates Thompson MS 26 is meant to supplement Baker's fundamental study and to question his conclusions concerning the patronage of the manuscript. See Baker, 'Medieval Illustrations'.

85 The Oxford manuscript has been placed in Durham through the contents, script and style of illuminations. However, Ker has identified an erased *ex libris* of the Augustinian priory at Southwick where it must have been at some point. See N. Ker, 'The

medieval home of the illustrated *Life of St. Cuthbert*', *Bodleian Library Record*, v, 1954, p. 6.

86 Otto Pächt, *The Rise of Pictorial Narrative in Twelfth-Century England* (Oxford, 1962). For a critique of Pächt see Cynthia Hahn, 'Picturing the Text', pp. 1–33.

87 M. Inguanez and M. Avery, *La Vita di S. Bennedetto*, Facsimile edition (Monte Cassino, 1934). For a discussion of the possible historical connections between these two manuscripts see Otto Pächt, *The Rise of Pictorial Narrative*, pp. 17ff.

88 William Noel, 'The Utrecht Psalter in England: Continuity and Experiment' in *The Utrecht Psalter in Medieval Art. Picturing the Psalms of David*, Koert van der Horst, William Noel and Wilhelmina C.M. Wüstefeld eds (London, 1996), pp. 120–165.

89 Margaret Gibson, T.A. Heslop, and Richard W. Pfaff eds, *The Eadwine Psalter. Text, Image, and Monastic Culture in Twelfth-Century Canterbury* (Pennsylvania, 1997).

90 *Durham Cathedral. A Celebration*, p. 107, fig. 71.

91 Malcolm Baker was unsure whether the missing folio between 13 and 14 would have carried an image prefacing chapter 4. Between folios 13 and 14 there is no text missing, therefore, if a folio was once there it would have had either an image and a blank folio or two back-to-back images. The confusion as to its existence may be due to the fact that the conjoint leaf is folio 20, a leaf that has been misplaced and has therefore caused the text to run in the incorrect sequence. If the conjoint leaf were to be placed in its correct position it would have carried its partner in the correct position just prior to chapter 4, providing space for two illuminations.

92 For example, there is concern for Cuthbert's charity, not his powers of prophecy, in the illustrations to Chapter 12, and the illustrations to Chapter 6 emphasize the relationship between Cuthbert and Boisil, which may, Baker argues, reflect interest in Ailred of Rievaulx's discussion of *amicitia*. This proposal is strengthened when one is reminded that Reginald of Durham dedicated his *Libellus* to Ailred of Rievaulx and that Ailred was originally from Durham.

93 See R.A.B. Mynors, 'The Stonyhurst Gospels: Textual Description and History of the Manuscript' in *Relics*, p. 358, note 1.

94 Letter 290 in *Monumeuta Germaniae Historica*, Epistolae, iv, pp. 448–9.

95 For a discussion of the meaning of patterned backgrounds see Sixten Ringbom, 'Some pictorial conventions for the recounting of thoughts and experiences in late medieval art' in *Medieval Iconography and Narrative. A Symposium* (Odense, 1980), pp. 38–69.

96 Baker, 'Medieval Illustrations', p. 36.

97 Baker, 'Medieval Illustrations', p. 36.

98 Baker has argued that the inclusion of the scene was directly related to the ecclesiastical political situation in Durham in the late twelfth century. The illustration of this event was unusual and therefore must have had some special significance. He suggested that the emphasis placed on Cuthbert's acceptance of the bishopric in this manuscript was closely tied with the dispute at Durham concerning the right of free election of the prior. However, the only link between these two issues, that is the election of the prior and the bishop, is the notion of a fair election, rather than the practice of simony. See Baker, 'Medieval Illustrations', p. 36–37.

99 Like the Galilee bishop, the figure stands frontally with his right hand blessing and in his left hand he holds a similar white crozier (perhaps with a gold band). He also wears the vestments of the Mass and carries a maniple. His white mitre has ornamented strips of gold although the hanging bands are not visible. As well, in both, there has been an attempt to frame the figures by enclosing them in large areas of colour. The Galilee bishop is set within an arched frame on a blue and green background, while the Cuthbert image is set within a rectangular frame on a gold and blue background.

100 For a discussion of this image see John Higgitt, 'Glastonbury, Dunstan, monasticism and manuscripts', *Art History*, Vol. 2, No. 3, 1979, pp. 275–290.

101 *The Rule of St Benedict*, Justin McCann trans. (London, 1976).

102 Chapter 58 deals with the order for the reception of brethren, in other words the ceremony of accepting a new novice. The final act of acceptance in this ceremony is the prostration of the novice before the feet of each monk, while asking him to pray for him. In Chapter 53, it recounts the proper way in which guests are to be received. The monk is to bow his head or even prostrate himself before the guest, 'so that Christ may be worshipped in them'. Chapter 67 requires that a monk, upon returning from a journey, lie prostrate on the floor of the oratory at the end of each canonical hour of work, and ask for prayers for all that they may have seen, heard or encountered on their trip. Chapters 71 and 44 deal with the manner in which a monk is to be punished. If a senior monk is offended by a more junior monk, for 'however trifling a reason', the junior monk is to cast himself down at his feet and make reparation. And finally, most seriously, if a monk has been excommunicated from the oratory and table, he is to lie prostrate at the door of the oratory, face down and at the feet of his brethren and say nothing until the abbot signals him to rise. He is then to throw himself at the feet of the abbot, then at his brethren's feet and ask them to pray for him.

103 A.J. Piper, 'The Durham Cantor's Book (Durham, Dean and Chapter Library, MS B.IV.24)' in *AN-D*, pp. 79–92.

104 Cynthia Hahn, 'Picturing the Text', pp. 1–33.

Select Bibliography

Abou-El-Haj, Barbara, *The Medieval Cult of Saints. Formations and Transformations*, Cambridge, 1997.

——, 'The Audience for the Medieval Cult of Saints', *Gesta*, XXX/1, 1991, pp. 3–15.

Aird, William M., *St. Cuthbert and the Normans. The Church of Durham, 1071–1153*, Woodbridge, 1998.

Backhouse, Janet, *The Lindisfarne Gospels*, Oxford, 1981.

Baker, M., 'Medieval Illustrations of Bede's *Life of St. Cuthbert*', *Journal of the Warburg and Courtauld Institutes*, 41, 1978, pp. 16–49.

Battiscombe, C.F. ed., *The Relics of St. Cuthbert*, Oxford, 1956.

Bonner, Gerald *et al* eds., *St. Cuthbert, His Cult and His Community to AD 1200*, Woodbridge, Suffolk, 1989.

Brown, Michelle P., *Understanding Illuminated Manuscripts. A Guide to Technical Terms*, London & Malibu, 1994.

Clanchy, M.T., *England and its Rulers 1066–1272*, London, 1983.

Coldstream, Nicola and Draper, Peter, Hon. eds., *Medieval Art and Architecture at Durham Cathedral*, British Archaeological Association Conference Transactions, III, 1977/1980.

Colgrave, Bertram, *Two Lives of Saint Cuthbert*, Cambridge, 1940.

——, 'The History of British Museum Additional MS. 39943', *English Historical Review*, Vol. LIV, No. CCXVI, 1939 pp. 673–677.

——, 'The Post-Bedan Miracles and Translations of St Cuthbert', *The Early Cultures of North-West Europe, H.M. Chadwick Memorial Studies*, ed. Sir C. Fox and B. Dickens, Cambridge, 1950, pp. 307–32.

Colgrave, Hilda, *Saint Cuthbert of Durham*, Durham, 1947.

Craster, H.E., 'The patrimony of St. Cuthbert', *English Historical Review*, 69, 1954.

Crosby, Everett U, *Bishop and Chapter in Twelfth-Century England*, Cambridge, 1994.

Dodds, M.H., 'The little book of the birth of St Cuthbert', *Archaeologia Aeliana*, Fourth series, vi, 1929, pp. 52–94.

Forbes-Leith, W., *The Life of St Cuthbert*, Edinburgh, 1888.

Jewell, Helen M., *The North-South Divide. The Origins of Northern Consciousness in England*, Manchester; New York, 1994.

Kauffmann, C.M., 'Manuscript Illumination at Worcester in the eleventh and twelfth centuries', BAACT, 1975/1978, pp. 43–50.

——, *Romanesque Manuscripts, 1066–1190. A Survey of Manuscripts Illuminated in the British Isles*, Vol. 3, London, 1975.

Ker, Neil R., *Books, Collectors and Libraries: Studies in Medieval Heritage*, London, 1985.

——, *English Manuscripts in the Century after the Norman Conquest*, Oxford, 1960.

——, From 'Above top line' to 'Below top line': A Change in Scribal Practice', *Celtica*, 5, 1960, pp. 13–16.

——, 'The medieval home of the illustrated *Life of St. Cuthbert*', *Bodleian Library Record*, v, 1954.

Longstaffe, W.H.D., 'Bishop Pudsey's Buildings in the present County of Durham', *Transactions of the Architectural and Archaeological Society of Durham and Northumberland*, ii, 1870, 1ff.

Marner, Dominic, 'The Bible of Hugh of le Puiset (Durham Cathedral Library, MS A.II.1)', *Anglo-Norman Durham 1093–1193*, Woodbridge, 1994, David Rollason *et al* eds., pp. 471–484.

——, *The Bible of Hugh du Puiset: Authority, Appropriation and Invention in the Late-Twelfth Century*, Ph.D. thesis, University of East Anglia, 1995.

McKeehan, I.P., 'The Book of the Nativity of St. Cuthbert', *Publications of the Modern Language Association*, xlviii, 1933, pp. 981–99.

Morgan, N., *Early Gothic Manuscripts I, 1190–1250. A Survey of Manuscripts Illuminated in the British Isles*, Vol. 4, London, 1982.

Mynors, R.A.B., *Durham Cathedral Manuscripts to the End of the Twelfth Century*, Durham, 1939.

Piper, A.J., 'The libraries of the monks of Durham', *Medieval Scribes, Manuscripts and Libraries*, M.B. Parkes and Andrew G. Watson eds., pp. 251–278.

Pocock, Douglas ed., *Durham Cathedral. A Celebration*, Durham, 1993.

Reginald of Durham, *Libellus de admirandis Beati Cuthberti Virtutibus*, J. Raine ed., SS, 1, 1835.

Rollason, D.W., 'Why was St Cuthbert so Popular?', *Cuthbert Saint and Patron*, Durham, 1987, pp. 9–22.

——, Margaret Harvey and Michael Prestwich eds, *Anglo-Norman Durham 1093–1193*, Woodbridge, 1994.

Scammell, G.V., *Hugh du Puiset Bishop of Durham*, Cambridge, 1956.

Thacker, Alan, 'Bede's Ideal of Reform', *Ideal and Reality in Frankish and Anglo-Saxon Society*, P. Wormald ed., Oxford, 1983.

Tudor, Victoria, 'The Misogyny of Saint Cuthbert', *Archaeologia Aeliana*, 5th series, 12, 1984, pp. 157–67.

Vita S. Cuthberti Metrica, W. Jaager ed., *Palaestra*, 198, 1935.

White, W., 'The Galilee', *Royal Institute of British Architects*, Transactions, New. Ser., vi, 1890, 153–64.

Index

Adam 12
Aelfflaed 7
Aethelstan, King of England 9, 17, 19
Ailred of Rievaulx 44
alb 14, 30
Alcuin 46
Aldred 15
Alexander III, Pope 25
Alfred, King of England 9, 18
Amalarius of Metz 51
anonymous author, the *Life* of Cuthbert 11, 12
Asser 18

Bamburgh 17
Basan, Eadui 52
Bede 11, 30, 31, 40, 43, 44, 47
Benedictine monasticism 23, 32ff.
Bernician dynasty 17, 18
Boisil 7, 12, 43ff., 47

Canterbury Cathedral 24, 29, 31, 34, 55
Carlisle Cathedral 38
Chapel of the Nine Altars 29
chasuble 14, 30
Chester-le-Street 17, 33
Cluny, third abbey church 20
Cnut, King of England 9
Constitutions of Clarendon 25
crozier 30

dalmatic 14, 30
Danelaw 18
Deirian dynasty 17
Durham Library Catalogues 37
Durham Cathedral 9, 17, 18, 20, 23, 32, 33, 34, 37, 54, 55

Eadfrith 15
Eardwulf 15
Ebba, Abbess of Coldingham 31
Ecgfrith, King of Northumbria 7, 9, 13
Eugenius, bishop of Ardmore 35

Farne Island 9, 13, 14, 19, 23, 32, 34, 42, 46

Fitzherbert, William, archbishop of York 22, 23, 46
Flambard, bishop of Durham 22, 23, 45
Forcer, Johannis 38

Galilee Chapel 26, 27, 31, 33, 36, 38, 51, 54
Geoffrey of Coldingham 27
Good Friday 51ff.
Gospel of St John 22, 23, 45
Gregory of Tours, Pope 11, 44, 53

Haliwerfolc 19
Henry II, King of England 24ff.
Henry of Blois, bishop of Winchester 26
Henry of Huntingdon 18
hermitage 9, 13, 42, 47
Hugh du Puiset, bishop of Durham 22ff. 26, 29ff. 35, 37, 49, 51, 53, 54
Humber 18

Imitatio Christi 44

Jerusalem 12, 27
John of Salisbury 46

Kepier river 31

Lady Chapel 27ff.
Langley, Thomas 38
Lawson of Brough, Henry 38
Lawson, Isabelle 38
Lindisfarne 9, 11, 13, 14, 19, 20, 32, 42, 53

maniple 30
Manuscripts:
Biblioteca Apostolica Vaticana, cod. lat. 1202, *Life* of St Benedict and St Maur 41
British Library Cotton Nero D.iv, Lindisfarne Gospels 9, 15, 20, 22, 37
British Library Arundle MS 155, Rule of St Benedict 52

British Library Yates Thompson MS 26, *Life* of St Cuthbert 37ff.
British Library (loan), Cuthbert Gospel of St John 22, 46
Cambridge, Corpus Christi College MS. 183, Life of St Cuthbert 17
Cambridge, Trinity College MS B.16.3, de laudibus sanctus crucis 51
Cambridge, Trinity College, MS. R.17.1, Eadwine Psalter 43
Copenhagen Royal Library MS Thott. 143 2°, Copenhagen Psalter 39
Durham Cathedral Library MS A.II.1, Puiset Bible 38
Durham Cathedral Library MS A.II.19, Glossed Pauline Epistle 38
Durham Cathedral Library MS B.II.13, Glossed Psalms 43
Durham Cathedral Library MS B.IV.24, Monastic Constitutions of Lanfranc 52
Durham Cathedral Library MS B.IV.35, *Life* of St Cuthbert 39
Leiden, University Library, MS. Lat. 76A, Leiden Psalter 39
Oxford University College MS 165, *Life* of St Cuthbert 41, 42, 44, 47, 49
Oxford. Bodleian Library, Douce MS 270, Sermons of Maurice de Sully 39
Paris, Bibliothèque Nationale, MS. Lat. 8846 42
Utrecht University Library MS. 32, Utrecht Psalter 32, 41, 42

Margaret, Queen of Scotland 23
married clergy 33
Martyrologies 9
Maurus, Hrabanus 51
Melrose Abbey 7, 12, 35, 44 45
misogyny 32
mitre 30
Muriadach, King of Ireland 35

Norman Conquest 34, 41
Northumbria 15ff., 29ff., 34, 35

Papal Bull 51
Pastoral Care 18
Patrimony of St Cuthbert 19
pectoral cross 9, 14
pilgrimage 25, 31
pilgrims 31, 33, 36, 51, 54
pilgrim flasks 51
Prior Bertram 39
Prior Lawrence 44, 51
Prior Thomas 26, 48, 51
Prior Roger 23
'Proskynesis' 51

Quire(s) 40, 45

Raine, James 38, 55
Ranulf 20
Reginald of Durham 22, 23, 31ff.,
    44, 47, 54, 55;
Libellus 31, 32, 33, 36
Richard Bell, bishop of Carlisle
    38
Richard, King of England 30
Richard le Scrope 37
Ripon 12
Robert, scribe 43

Rudd, Thomas 38
Rule of St Benedict 52

Sabina 35
sarchophagus 14, 18
'Secundo folio' 37
St Augustine of Hippo 12, 22, 43
St Bartholomew 23
St Benedict 12, 52
St Bernard of Clairvaux 23
St Cuthbert:
and the North 17-19
and Reginald 31-33, 36
career 12-16
incorrupt body of 14, 22
Lives of 11-13
miracles 40ff.
representations of 29-31, 49ff.
St Edmund 9, 32, 33
St Etheldreda 32, 33
St Giles 31
St Godric of Finchale 23, 31, 33,
    34, 36, 54, 55
St John the Evangelist 12, 23
St Lawrence, church of , Pitting-
    ton 30
St Malachy, bishop of Armagh 23
St Martin of Tours 12, 18
St Nicholas of Bari 23

St Oswald 17, 23, 26, 30, 31
St Thomas Becket 9, 23, 24, 31,
    32ff., 54, 55
St Wilfrid 18
Speyer Cathedral 20
Stephanus, Eddius 18
Stephen, King of England 26
stole 30
Stubbs, William 26
Symeon of Durham 17, 22, 23, 40
Synod 13, 49, 50

Tees 17, 20
Theobald of Bec 25
Tynemouth 18

Urban III, Pope 51

Verca, Abbess 14
Vikings 15

William of Malmesbury 18
William of St Calais 17, 33
William of Sens 29
William the Conqueror 20
Wulfhere of Mercia 18

Yates Thompson, Henry 37, 38
York Cathedral 38